AEPSi™ Provider Guide

Baltimore • London • Sydney

Paul H. Brookes Publishing Co.
Post Office Box 10624
Baltimore, MD 21285-0624

www.brookespublishing.com

Copyright © 2013 by Paul H. Brookes Publishing Co., Inc.
All rights reserved.

"Paul H. Brookes Publishing Co." is a registered trademark of
Paul H. Brookes Publishing Co., Inc.

"AEPS®" is a registered trademark and AEPSi™, AEPS™, and AEPSi™ are trademarks of Paul H. Brookes Publishing Co., Inc.

Manufactured in the United States of America by
Bradford & Bigelow, Newburyport, Massachusetts.

No real personal information is represented in any text or illustration in this guide. Any relation to true personal information is coincidental, and no inferences are intended.

For technical support for AEPSi, please call 1-866-386-2666 or e-mail techsupport@brookespublishing.com.

To contact the AEPSi Implementation Team, please e-mail implementation@brookespublishing.com.

For information regarding training, please call 1-866-386-2666 ext. 2 or e-mail seminars@brookespublishing.com.

Version 1.1

ISBN-13 978-1-59857-392-3
ISBN-10 1-59857-392-6

2017   2016   2015
10   9   8   7   6   5   4   3

Contents

Introduction	**1**
About AEPSi	1
About the *AEPSi™ Provider Guide*	1
Section 1: Logging In	**2–3**
Forgotten Username or Password	3
Section 2: My AEPSi	**4–5**
My Children	4
Calendar	4
What's New	4
Messages	4
Assessments in Progress	4
My Reports	5
Section 3: My Children	**5–6**
Add a New Child	5–6
• Creating a Child Profile	6
Section 4: Child Summary	**7–8**
Profile	7
Recent Activity	7
Calendar	7
AEPS Tests	7
Child Journal Recent Entries	8
Family Reports	8
Child Reports	8
Section 5: Child Profile	**9**
Section 6: Child Calendar	**10–11**
Adding a Calendar Entry	10
Viewing/Editing/Deleting a Calendar Entry	11
Printing Calendar	11
Section 7: Child Journal	**12**
Adding a Child Journal Entry	12
Section 8: Child Team	**13**
Section 9: Child Assessments	**14–22**
Creating a New CODRF	14–19
• CODRF Summary Page	14–16
▪ CODRF Summary	15
▪ Accessing the AEPSi Curriculum Reference Guide	15
▪ Selecting Test Areas	16
▪ OSEP Include	16

- Filling in a CODRF 17–18
- Viewing/Printing/Editing/Deleting/Exporting a CODRF 19
- Copy Scores from Previous Assessment 19

Customized CODRFs 20–21
- Scores 21
- Notes 21
- Include Items Marked IFSP/IEP 21

Child Outcomes Summary Form (COSF) 21–22
- Create Child Outcomes Summary Form 22
- View/Print/Edit/Delete Child Outcomes Summary Form 22

Section 10: Family Report 23–24

Entering a New Family Report 23
Sections of the Family Report 24
- Activities 24
- Fine Motor, Gross Motor, Adaptive, Social-Communication, and Social 24
- Cognitive 24
- Intervention Priorities 24

Viewing/Printing/Editing/Deleting a Family Report 24

Section 11: Child Reports 25–30

Score Summary 25
Graphed Scores 25–26
Child Progress Record 26
Provider Notes 27
IFSP/IEP Summary 27
Eligibility Cutoff Scores 28
Present Level of Functioning 28
Running Reports in Spanish 29
Create Custom Child Report 29–30
- Scores 30
- Notes 30
- Include Items Marked IFSP/IEP 30

Section 12: My Groups 31–35

Creating a Group 31
Group Assessment Summary 32–34
- Editing a Group Assessment 33
- Deleting a Group 34

Creating a Group Journal Entry 34–35
- Editing/Deleting a Group Journal Entry 35

Section 13: My Calendar 36

Section 14: My Reports 37–50

Child Reports 37
Aggregate Reports 38–50
- Class Reports 38
- Group Snapshots Reports 38–43
  - Status of All Children Report 39
  - Progress of All Children Report 40
  - Group Goal Planning Matrix Report 41–42
  - Child Profile List Report 43

- OSEP Categories Reports 44–48
  - About OSEP Reporting 44
  - Children on the Alternative Path 44–45
  - Entry Data Only (Aggregate Percentages) Report 45
  - Entry Data Only (Categories for Each Child) Report 46
  - Progress Data (Aggregate Percentages) Report 46
  - Progress Data (Categories for Each Child) Report 47
  - OSEP Report Exclusion Categories 47–48
- ECO Child Outcomes Summary Form Ratings 49–50
  - Entry Data Only (Ratings for Each Child) Report 49
  - Progress Data (Ratings for Each Child) Report 50

Section 15: My Toolkit 51–52

Section 16: My Profile 53
  Editing My Profile 53

Section 17: Help 54

Introduction

About AEPSi

AEPSinteractive™ (AEPSi™) is a web-based management system for the *Assessment, Evaluation, and Programming System for Infants and Children (AEPS®), Second Edition*, that makes it easier for AEPS users to make the most of AEPS, meet reporting mandates, determine eligibility, and manage and track child data. AEPSi has all the integrity of AEPS plus the time- and paperwork-saving convenience of automated scoring and powerful functionality that transforms AEPS findings into Child Progress Reports and OSEP Child Outcomes Reports. AEPS is truly a complete solution for programs that also need to meet accountability and eligibility challenges—without sacrificing quality programming and good outcomes for children.

AEPSi makes it easier for you to help your children make real progress.

About the *AEPSi™ Provider Guide*

The *AEPSi™ Provider Guide* is intended to help you navigate and perform all functions of the AEPSi online tool. This manual for providers has been written with the basic AEPSi user in mind.

Who is an AEPSi user? AEPSi users can be early childhood professionals, service providers, or various team members—in short, anyone who is not an AEPSi Administrator. This guide is designed for users like you who are tasked with assessing children. You may be a preschool teacher, a teacher's aide, a home visitor, or a speech-language pathologist—and you may wear multiple hats in your professional life.

Within this guide, you will find basic information about how to enter child records, how to enter an assessment of a child or group of children using AEPS, and how to generate child and group reports based on assessment results. This, however, is just the beginning. You'll also find detailed instructions on how to navigate through each area of AEPSi.

Thank you for choosing AEPSi as your online assessment and intervention tool.

Logging In   Section 1

The AEPSi login page is where you log in to access your AEPSi account. You may also follow the tabbed links at the top of the page to access additional information about AEPS and AEPSi. Logging in to AEPSi is the first step to setting up your personalized AEPSi account. As a new user, you should receive an e-mail generated by AEPSi that contains your username and a link to set up your password.

> From: Brookes Publishing
> Sent: Wednesday, May 01, 2013 3:10 PM
> To: Monica Belle
> Subject: AEPSi Account Information: Account Information.
>
> Dear Monica Belle,
>
> Please select the following link (or copy and paste the link into the address bar of your web browser) in order to set or change your AEPSi password:
>
> https://www.aepsi.com/aepsi/passwordchange.htm?p1=384444&p2=78690&p3=621&p4=377962&sla=no
>
> Once you have accepted the terms of the end user license agreement and created your password, you will be taken to the AEPSi login page where you will enter your username and new password.
>
> Your username is: mbelle525.
>
> If you have any questions about setting your password, please contact the person at your program who has been designated AEPSi Administrator, or contact Technical Support at 1-866-386-2666 or email techsupport@brookespublishing.com
>
> AEPSi Customer Support
> http://www.aepsi.com
>
> Please do not reply to this e-mail.

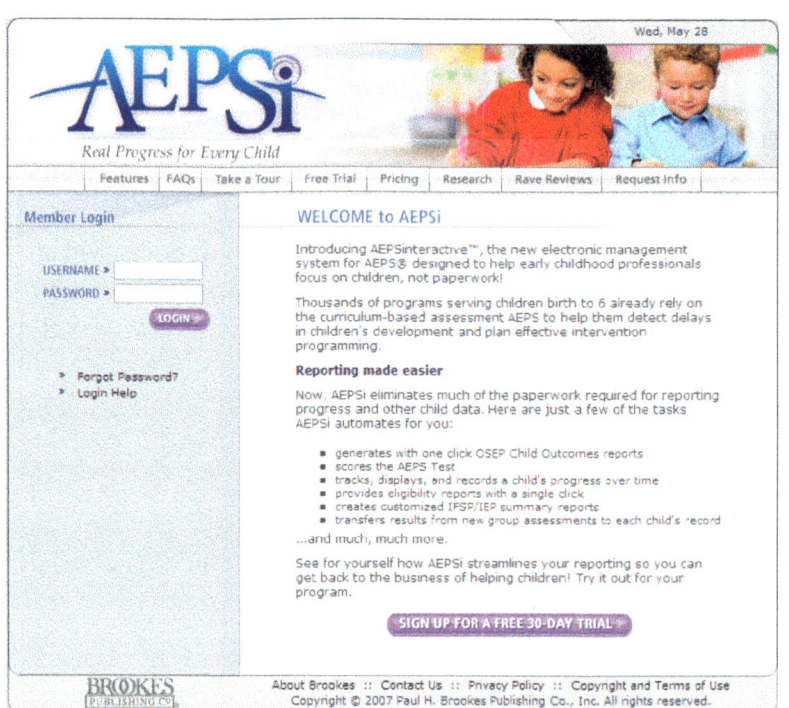

Once you're an AEPSi user, type in the AEPSi URL (**www.aepsi.com**) and you will be directed to the **Login** page.

Enter your username and password, and click the *Login* button to enter the AEPSi site.

> Note: It is very important that you log off when you are finished using AEPSi. To log off, click Log Off on the upper right-hand corner from any screen within AEPSi. If you fail to log off and you use a public computer, other people who use the computer may be able to see your private AEPSi information, including child names and records.

Forgotten Username or Password

If you have forgotten your password, click on the *Forgot Password?* link on the AEPSi home page (**www.aepsi.com**).

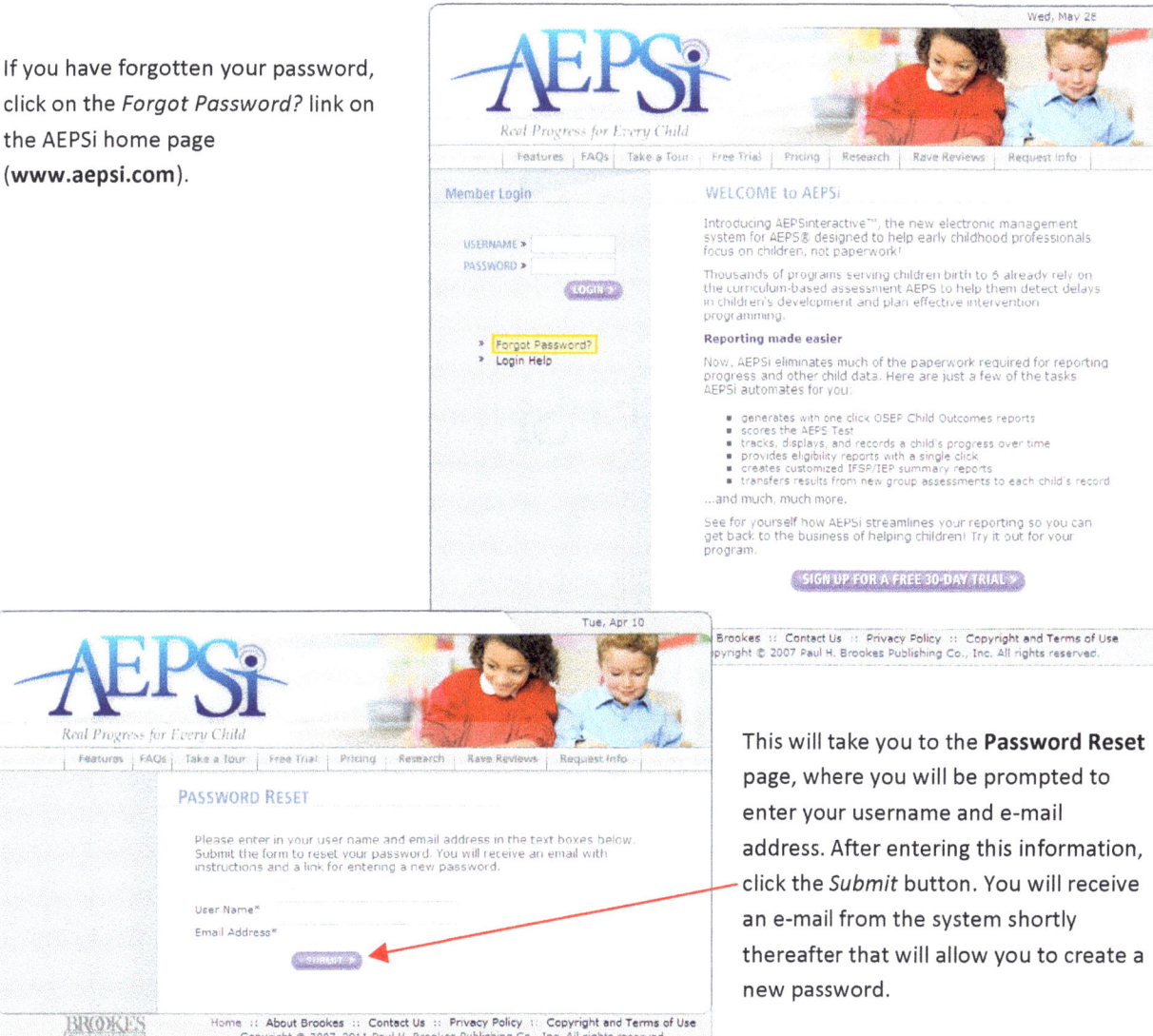

This will take you to the **Password Reset** page, where you will be prompted to enter your username and e-mail address. After entering this information, click the *Submit* button. You will receive an e-mail from the system shortly thereafter that will allow you to create a new password.

If you have forgotten your username, click on the *Forgot Username?* link on the AEPSi home page (**www.aepsi.com**). Enter your e-mail address and click the *Submit* button. You will receive an e-mail from the system with your username(s).

My AEPSi

Section 2

My AEPSi is your personalized homepage within the AEPSi system. It is designed to give you a snapshot of your activity and options within AEPSi. You will always be directed to this page when you log in. From **My AEPSi**, you can click links that are on the taskbar at the top of the screen (**My Children, My Groups, My Reports, My Calendar, My Toolkit, My Profile,** and **Help**), and under the subheadings **My Children, Calendar, What's New, Messages, Assessments in Progress,** and **My Reports**.

My Children

My Children shows you a snapshot of children to whom you are assigned. To view all children in your AEPSi, click *View All*. To add a new child from this page, click the *Add New Child* button.

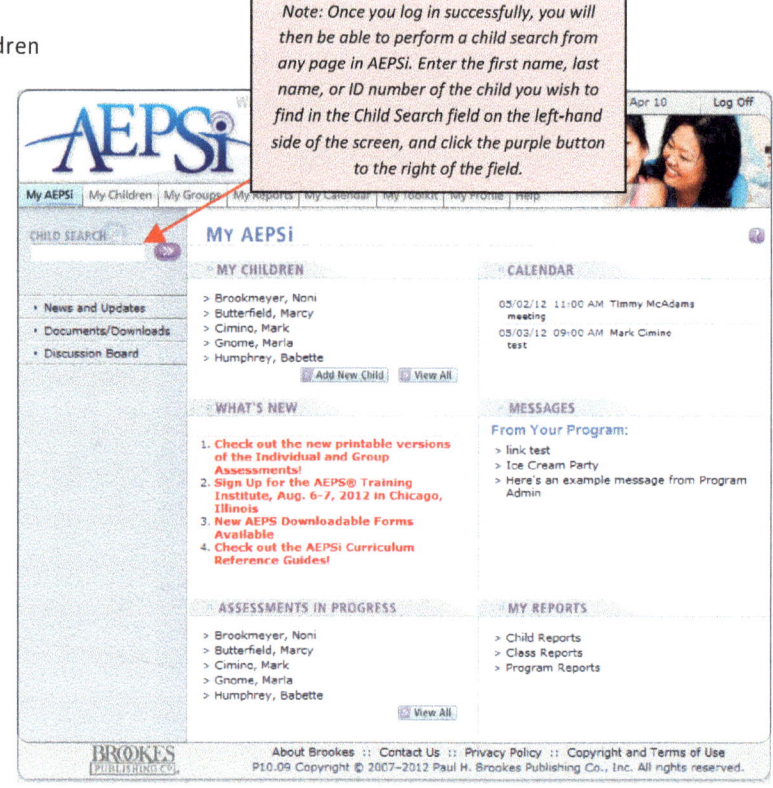

Note: Once you log in successfully, you will then be able to perform a child search from any page in AEPSi. Enter the first name, last name, or ID number of the child you wish to find in the Child Search field on the left-hand side of the screen, and click the purple button to the right of the field.

Calendar

The **Calendar** section in your **My AEPSi** page shows a short list of events for which you have been marked as an attendee, starting with today's date. Click on the event title to see more information about that event. To view additional entries, click on the **My Calendar** tab at the top of the screen. You will be directed to the **My Calendar** page that lists all calendar events for which you have been marked as an attendee. See *Section 13: My Calendar* for more information on how to add or edit calendar events.

What's New

The **What's New** section highlights the most recent news and updates from Brookes Publishing Co., the developer of AEPSi. Keep an eye on this section to find out about updates to AEPSi designed to make your work easier.

Messages

Your Administrator has the ability to post messages that will appear under the **Messages** tab of your **My AEPSi** home page. If your program is part of an Enterprise account, you may also receive messages from the Enterprise Administrator. To view a message, click on the message name. A pop-up window will appear with the entire message.

Assessments in Progress

Assessments in Progress shows a short list of your children for whom assessments have been started but are not yet complete. They are listed by child name. You may continue to work on an assessment by selecting a child's name.

My Reports

My Reports provides quick links to Child Reports and Class Reports. Click either *Child Reports* or *Class Reports* to be directed to these areas. Note that if you are a Reviewer or Administrator, in addition to being a Provider, you will also see a link to *Program Reports* in this section.

My Children   Section 3

The **My Children** page is the central location where all children to whom you are assigned in AEPSi are listed. From here you can select a child and manage all of his or her information that has been entered into the AEPSi system.

By clicking the **My Children** tab at the top of the screen, you are brought to the **My Children** page, which contains a list of your children and their names, ID numbers, and status of last assessment. Your children will be grouped according to their assessment status and then arranged in alphabetical order according to last name.

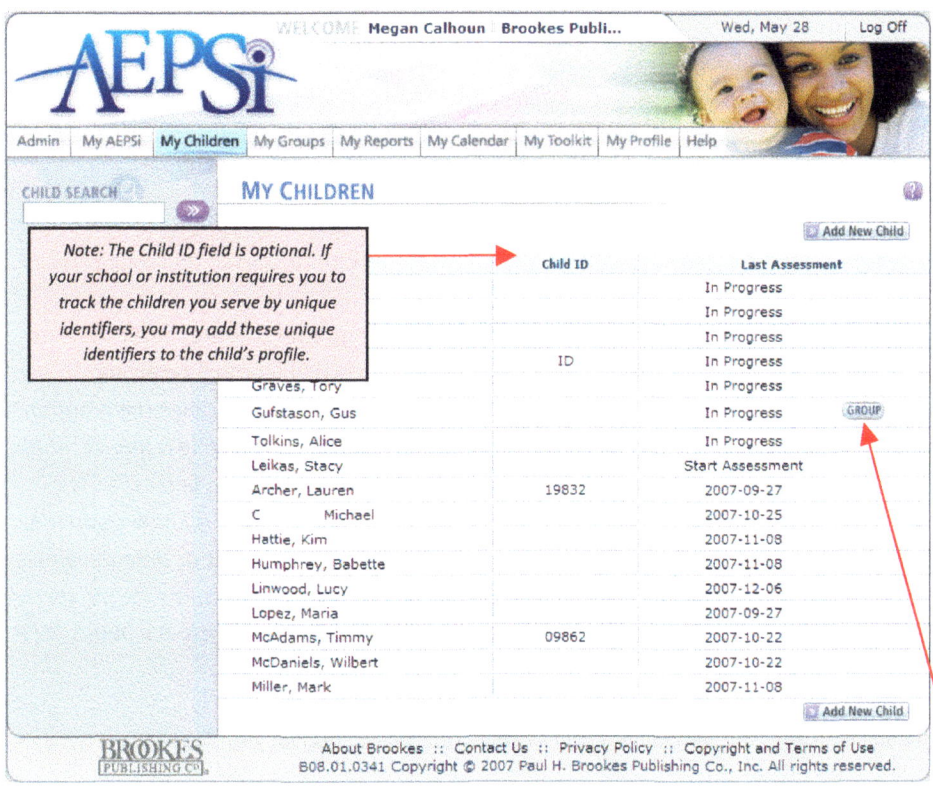

If the last assessment is incomplete, In Progress will be displayed in the Last Assessment column.

If a child has never been assessed, Start Assessment will be displayed in the Last Assessment column.

If the last assessment administered is complete, the date of that assessment will be shown in the Last Assessment column.

If a child is part of a group, you will see a group icon in the Last Assessment column.

Clicking any of the links in the Last Assessment column will take you to the **CODRF Summary** page. Clicking a child's name or Child ID from the **My Children** page will take you to that child's summary page, from which you may access all of his or her information, assessments, and reports.

Add a New Child

To add a child, click the *Add New Child* button from either the **My Children** section of your **My AEPSi** page or from the **My Children** page. You will be taken to the **Child Profile** page where you will be prompted to fill in information regarding the child.

Creating a Child Profile

When creating a new child profile, you will need to fill in key child information on the child record (e.g., first name, last name, date of birth). Required fields are indicated with a red arrow to the left of the field name.

The Administrator(s) of your program may create additional custom fields, which will appear on the bottom of the profile page.

In order for a child to be included in OSEP reporting, there are four required fields that must be completed:

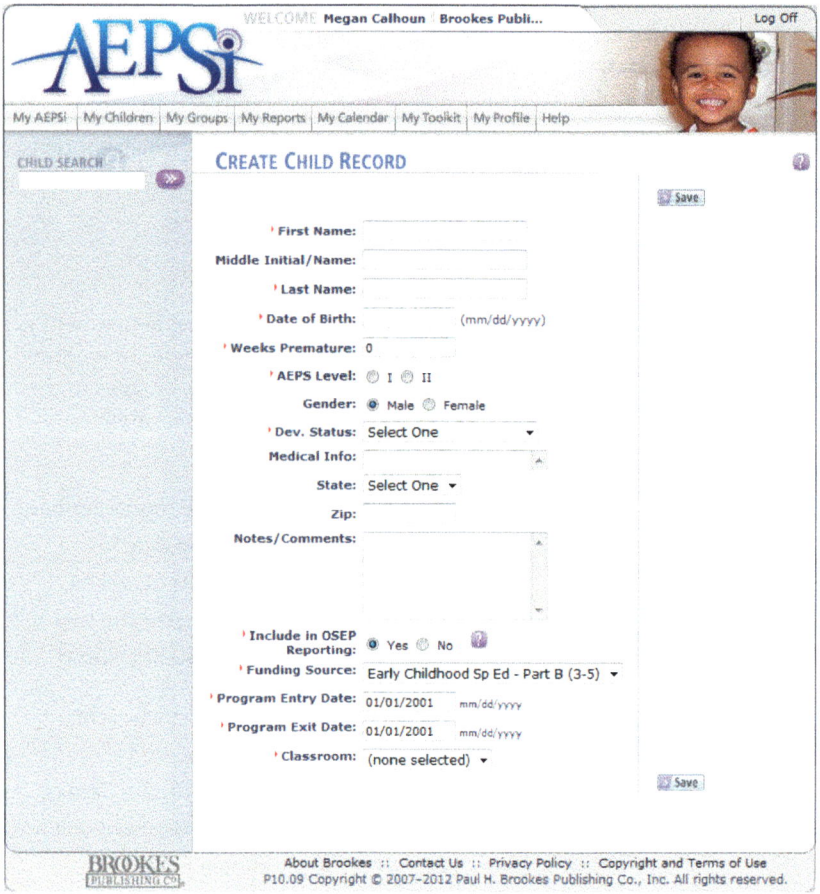

Include in OSEP Reporting: Select Yes if the child will be included in OSEP reporting. If the child will not be included in OSEP reporting, select No and leave the funding source, program entry date, and program exit date at their default values.

Funding Source: Select whether the child is Early Childhood Sp Ed - Part B (3–5) or Early Intervention - Part C (Birth–3).

Program Entry Date: Enter the date the child started receiving services.

Program Exit Date: Enter the date the child stopped receiving services. (*Note: Once the program exit date for a child is known, enter that information here. Until the child's exit date is known, you may leave the field at its default value. If a valid date is not entered, the child won't be included in the OSEP Exit Reports.*)

For information on viewing a child's profile, see **Section 5**: **Child Profile**. To add a Caregiver Profile, see **Section 8: Child Team**.

Child Summary

Section 4

The **Child Summary** page is the central place for managing a child's activity. The page also contains snapshots of the child's profile, recent changes made to his or her AEPSi records, calendar events, recent assessments, recent journal entries, and quick links to his or her individual Child Reports.

To get to the **Child Summary** page, select a child's name from the list on the **My Children** page.

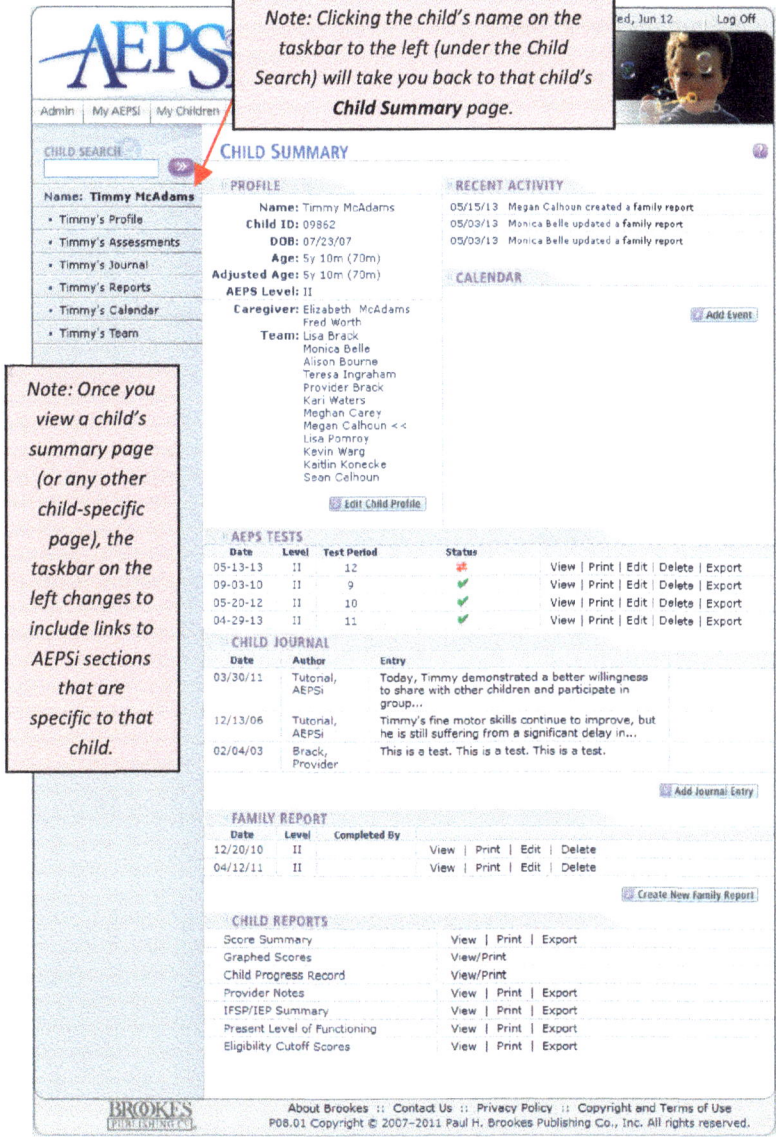

Profile

The Profile portion of the **Child Summary** page provides you with some of the basic information about the child and a list of the members of that child's team. To view or edit the child's complete profile, click the *Edit Child Profile* button or the *[Child's Name] Profile* link on the left taskbar. For more information about the child's profile **Section 8: Child Team**.

Recent Activity

The **Recent Activity** section shows you a list of the three most recently saved items for a child. You may click an item that includes the date and activity to view it.

Note: Calendar entries and child team changes will not appear in Recent Activity.

Calendar

The Calendar portion of the **Child Summary** page shows a list of events that are scheduled for the child, starting with today's date. To enter a new event, click the *Add Event* button or the *[Child's Name] Calendar* link on the left taskbar. For more information about the Child Calendar, see **Section 6: Child Calendar**.

AEPS Tests

In the middle of the **Child Summary** page, you will see a list of the child's most recent assessments under *AEPS Tests*. You may select an assessment from this list to view, print, edit, or export, or you may click the *Create New CODRF* button to begin a new assessment.

Clicking the *[Child's name]'s Assessments* from the left toolbar will give you access to all of this child's assessments. See **Section 9: Child Assessments** for more information on how to fill out new assessments or edit existing ones.

AEPSi Provider Guide | 7

Child Journal Recent Entries

Below the list of recent assessments is a list of a child's recent journal entries. You may view an entry by clicking the first several words of the entry or create a new entry by clicking the *Add Journal Entry* button. The *[Child's name]'s Journal* link on the left taskbar will take you to a page that shows all of the journal entries for that child.

Family Reports

Under the list of journal entries is a list of the child's Family Reports. You may select a Family Report to view, print, edit, or delete from this page or click on the *Create New Family Report* button to start a new Family Report. See **Section 10: Family Report**, for more information about the Family Report.

Child Reports

At the bottom of the **Child Summary** page are links to view, print, and export all of the available individual Child Reports. The *[Child's Name] Reports* link on the left task bar will take you to the **Child Reports** page where you will have access to all of these reports and more. See **Section 11: Child Reports**, for more information about Child Reports.

> *Note: Child Reports will only appear on the **Child Summary** page after at least one assessment has been finalized.*

Child Profile

Section 5

To view the child's complete profile, click the link to the left (e.g., *Timmy's Profile*).

Within the **Child Profile** is information on both the child and his or her caregivers(s).

When the **Child Profile** page is open, you may edit child information by clicking the *Edit Child Profile* button.

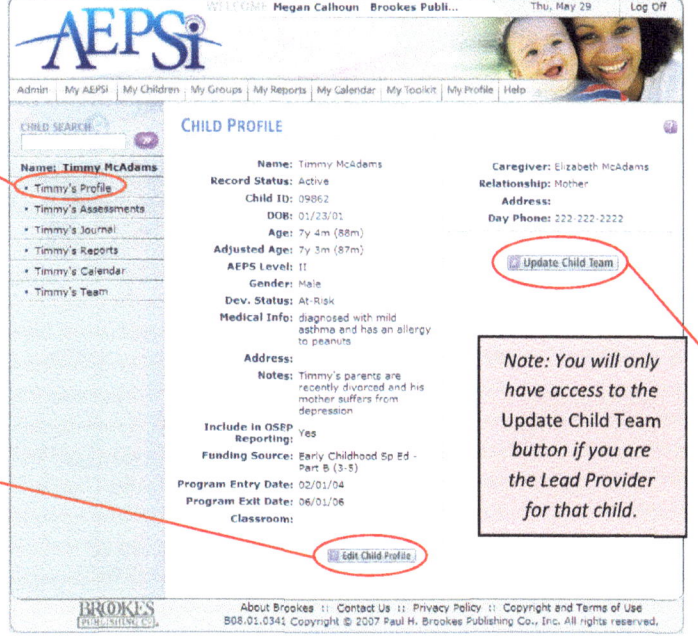

To add/edit caregiver information or update a child's team, click the *Update Child Team* button.

Note: You will only have access to the Update Child Team button if you are the Lead Provider for that child.

The **Update Child Team** page will contain a list of the child's team members once they are assigned to the child (the Child Team includes the caregiver[s]).

To add caregiver information to the child's profile, click the *Add Caregiver* button.

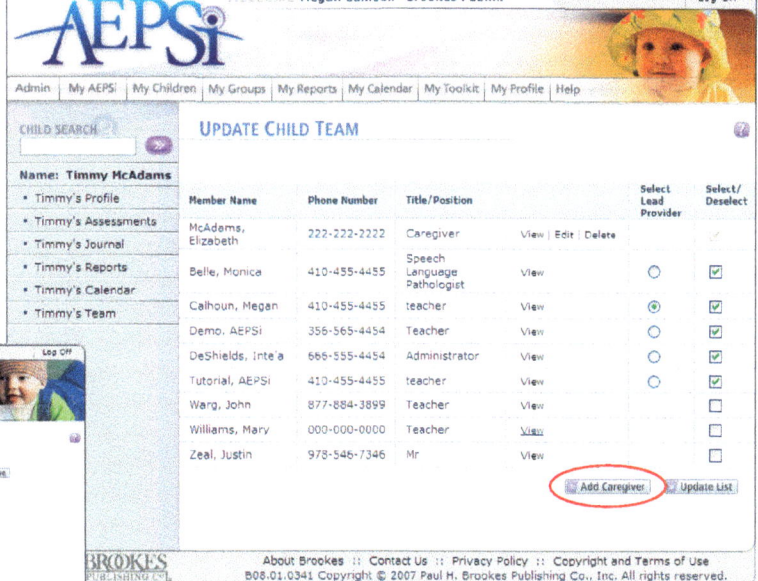

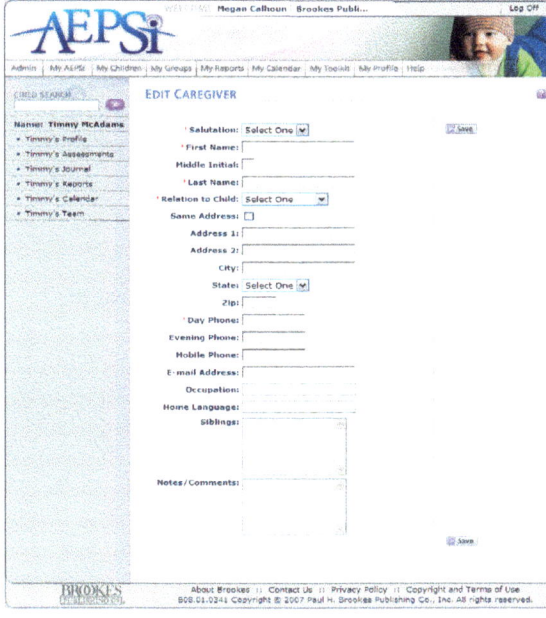

Fill out all required fields indicated by a red arrow and any additional fields. When you are done, click the *Save* button.

The caregiver will be saved as one of the child's team members, and you will return to the **Child Summary** page.

For more information about the child's team, see **Section 8: Child Team**.

Child Calendar

Section 6

To access a child's calendar, click on the link on the left task bar (e.g., *Timmy's Calendar*). This will take you to the **Child Calendar** page, where you will see a list of all of the upcoming events scheduled for the child starting with today's date.

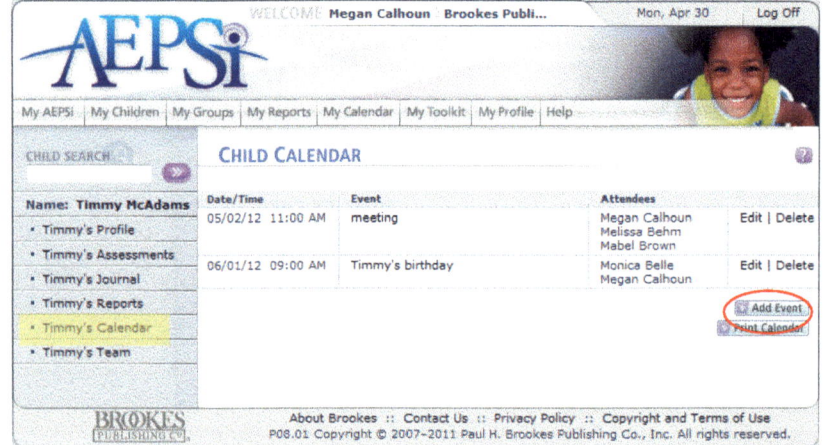

Adding a Calendar Entry

To add a calendar event, click the *Add Event* button from the **Child Summary** or **Child Calendar** pages. You will be taken to a screen to create a calendar.

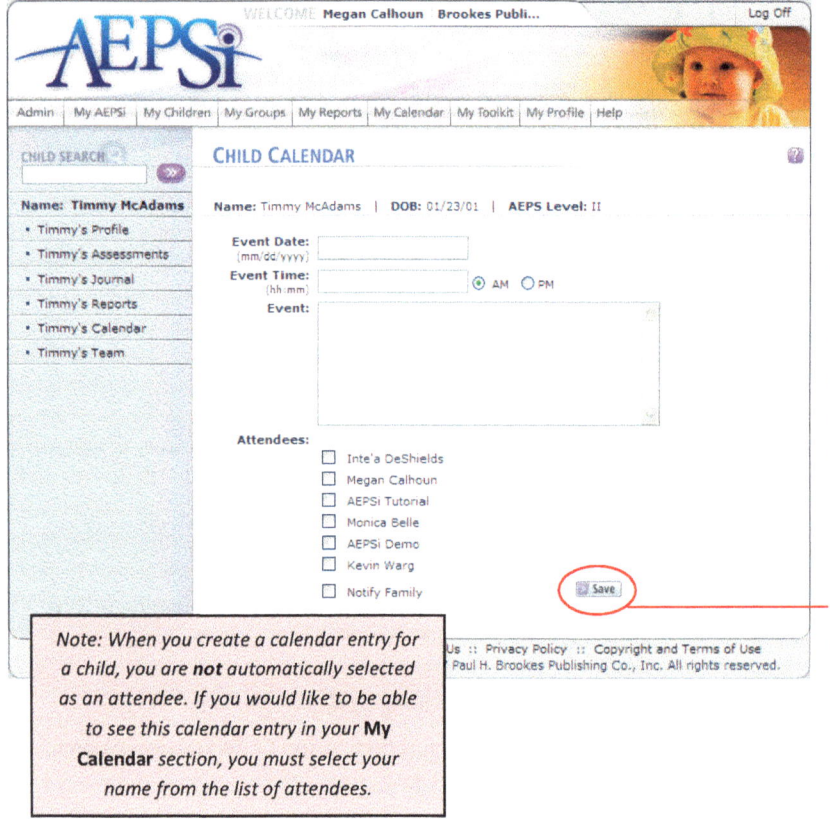

Enter the event date, time (select AM or PM), event, and attendees.

Click the *Notify Family* box if this is an event the family or caregiver(s) should be aware is taking place. (This does not send the family member an e-mail but serves as a reminder for the Provider when viewing the calendar.)

Click the *Save* button to save the event.

*Note: When you create a calendar entry for a child, you are **not** automatically selected as an attendee. If you would like to be able to see this calendar entry in your **My Calendar** section, you must select your name from the list of attendees.*

10 | AEPSi Provider Guide

Viewing/Editing/Deleting a Calendar Entry

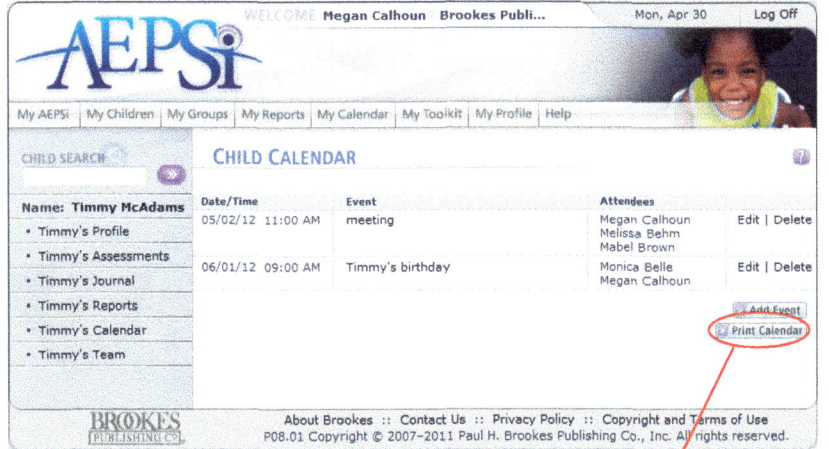

To view an event, click the date/time or event title of the event you would like to view from the **Child Summary** or **Child Calendar** pages.

To edit or delete an event, click the *Edit* or *Delete* links next to the calendar event for which you would like to perform this action on the **Child Calendar** page.

Printing Calendar

To print all events in a child's calendar, click the *Print Calendar* button at the bottom of the **Child Calendar** page.

To print a particular calendar entry, first view the entry by clicking the date/time or event title of the event and then clicking the *Print Event* button.

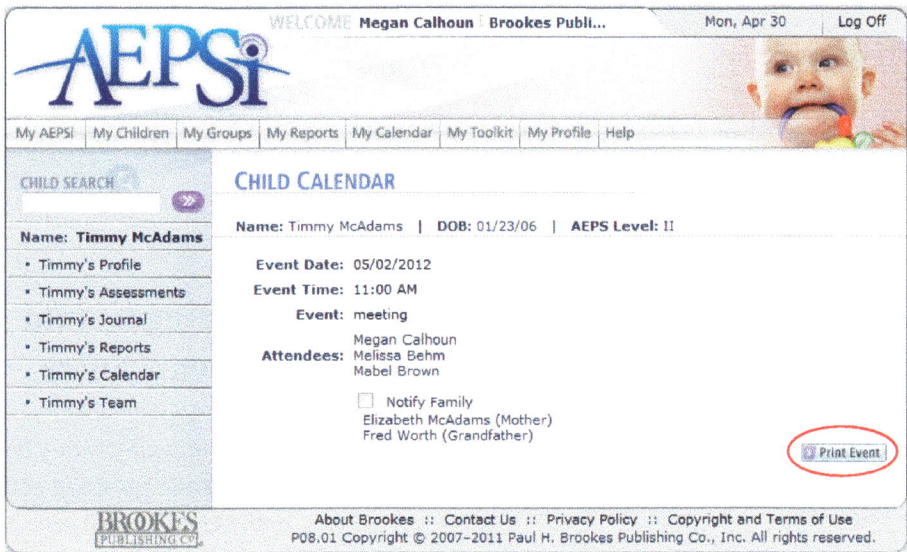

Child Journal

Section 7

Child journal entries are an effective way to make notes on a child's progress that can be shared with the child's other team members; these notes will be visible to each team member who is associated with this child and is an AEPSi user. This is also a good place to view other team members' entries on a specific child.

The **Child Journal** page, accessible from any of the child-specific pages by clicking a specific child's journal link on the taskbar to the left (e.g., *Timmy's Journal*), contains a chronological list of journal entries that shows the date, author, and the first few words of the entry.

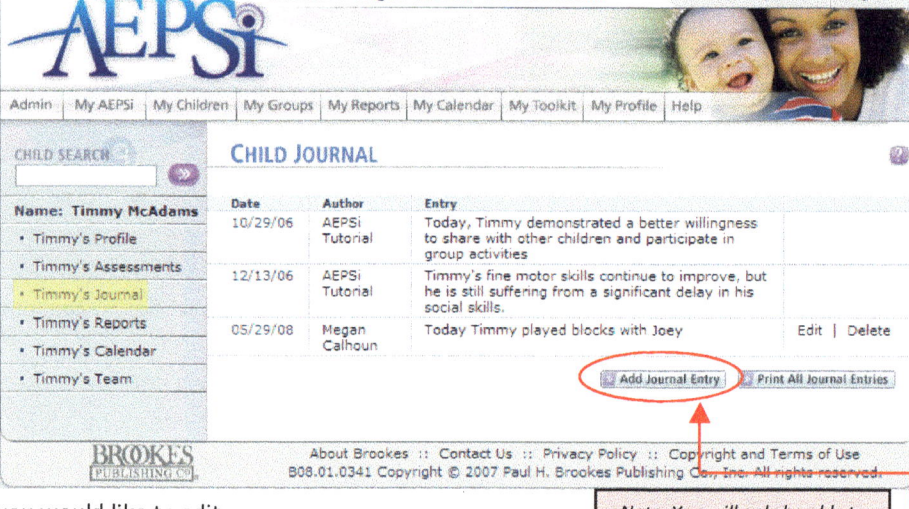

To view a complete journal entry, click the first few words of the entry.

To edit a journal entry, click *Edit* next to the entry you would like to edit.

Note: You will only be able to edit and delete journal entries that you originally entered.

To delete a journal entry, click *Delete* next to the entry you would like to delete.

To print an individual journal entry, first click the *Edit* link next to the entry and then click the *Print* button at the bottom of that entry's page.

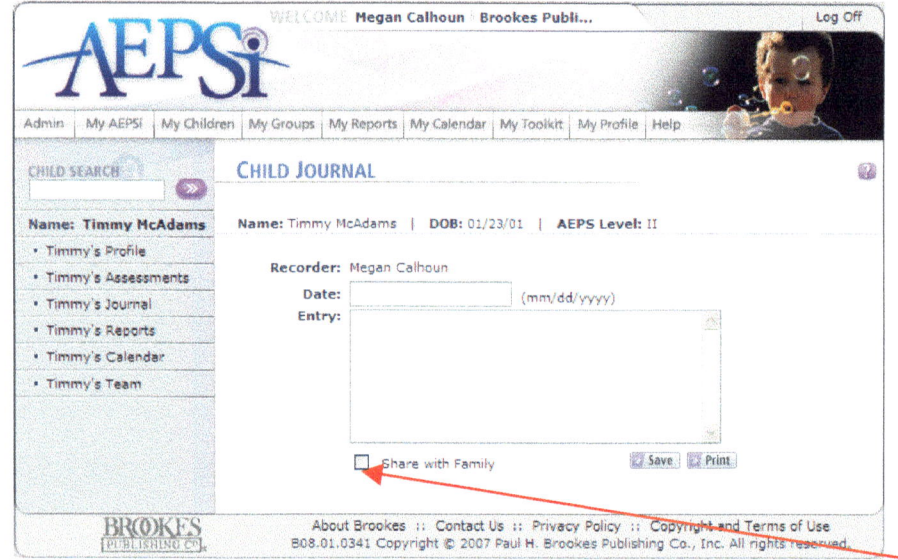

Adding a Child Journal Entry

To add a journal entry, click the *Add Journal Entry* button below the last listed entry on the **Child Journal** main page or on the **Child Summary** page. To add text, type inside the Entry text box.

To make other users aware that you approve having this entry shared with the child's caregiver(s), click the *Share with Family* box.

Click the *Save* button to save this entry.

12 | AEPSi Provider Guide

Child Team
Section 8

The **Child Team** page is the area within AEPSi where you can view, edit, and change a specific Child Team member. You can also view each team member's profile in this section.

The **Child Team** page, accessed by clicking a specific child's team link on the taskbar to the left (e.g., *Timmy's Team*), contains a list of that child's team members' names, e-mail addresses, phone numbers, and titles/positions.

To view individual team member information, click the team member's name from the **Child Team** page. You will be taken to a screen where you can see the member's profile information.

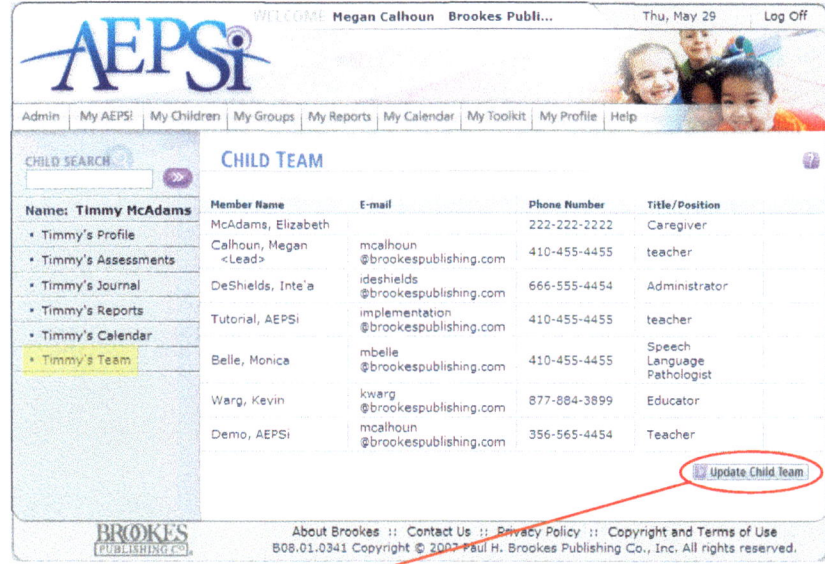

If you are a child's Lead Provider, you are able to make changes to a child's team through the *Update Child Team* button on the Child Team page. If you are not the child's Lead Provider, there will be no *Update Child Team* button on this page. To see who a child's Lead Provider is, look at the list of Providers next to Team under the Child Profile portion of the **Child Summary** page. On that page, the Lead Provider will be marked with <>. To update the list of team members, click the *Update Child Team* button below the last team member entry on the **Child Team** page.

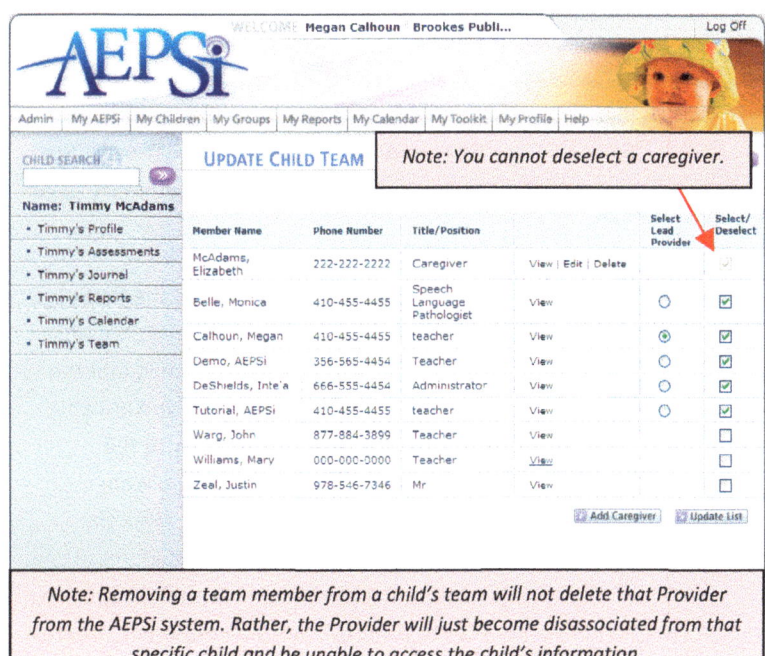

You may add or remove a team member by checking or unchecking the box under the Select/Deselect column next to that person's name and clicking the *Update List* button.

You may change the child's Lead Provider by selecting the radio button next to a team member's name under Select Lead Provider and clicking the *Update List* button.

> Note: A child may have only one Lead Provider.

You may add a caregiver by clicking the *Add Caregiver* button on the bottom of the **Update Child Team** page. Existing caregiver information may also be edited or deleted from the **Update Child Team** page by clicking the *Edit* or *Delete* link next to the caregiver's name at the top of the child's team list.

Child Assessments

Section 9

The **Child Assessments** page is the portal to AEPS assessments. By selecting a **Child Assessments** page from the left toolbar (e.g., *Jenny's Assessments*), you will be able to view all of this child's previously recorded assessments and fill out new assessments.

The **Child Assessments** page contains a list of all of the child's Child Observation Data Recording Forms (CODRFs) and Family Reports.

The CODRF listings are organized by the dates they were entered into AEPSi (which do not necessarily coincide with the dates the assessments were completed).

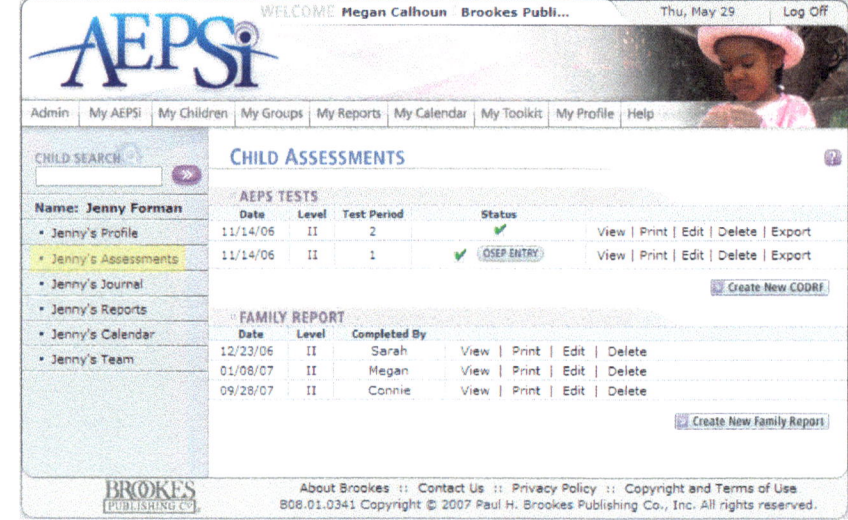

Information about the CODRFs included on this list is date, level, test period, and status (whether or not the CODRF is complete, if it is marked for OSEP reporting, and if it is a group assessment).

The Family Report listings are organized by date and show the level and person who completed the report.

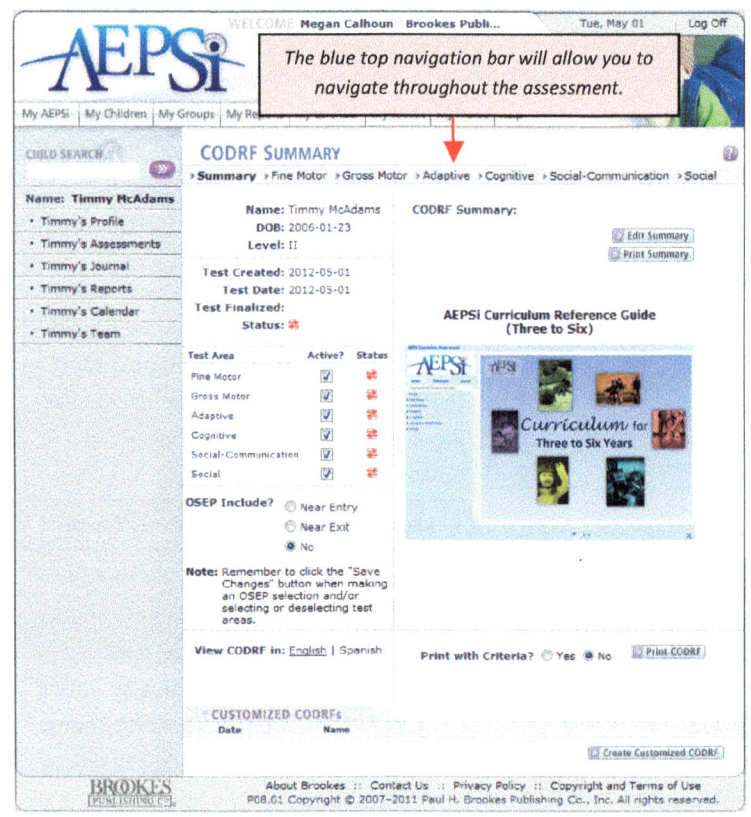

Creating a New CODRF

The CODRF is the form used to record a child's performance on the AEPS Test. To create a new CODRF, click the *Create New CODRF* button on either the **Child Summary** or **Child Assessments** page. You will be taken to the **CODRF Summary** page.

CODRF Summary Page

The **CODRF Summary** page is the first page of every child's assessment and contains brief information about the child and the assessment. From this page, you are able to enter a narrative summary of the CODRF, select which areas you want included on the assessment, mark the assessment for inclusion in OSEP reporting, choose to view the assessment in Spanish, opt to print the entire assessment, create a customized CODRF, and link to the AEPSi Curriculum Reference Guide.

14 | AEPSi Provider Guide

CODRF Summary

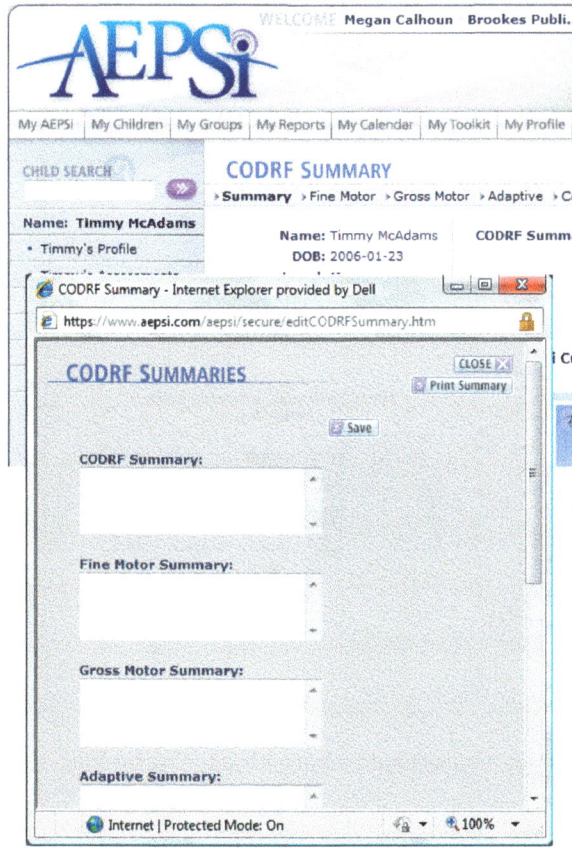

To create or edit a CODRF summary, click the *Edit Summary* button in the top right-hand corner of the **CODRF Summary** page.

A box will pop up that shows a place for the CODRF Summary and each domain's summary. Click inside each text box to add a summary. Click the *Save* button to save your changes or the *Print Summary* button to print the CODRF Summary. To close the pop-up box, click the *Close* button at the top or bottom of the pop-up. You are also able to print the CODRF Summary directly from the **CODRF Summary** page.

Note: You also are able to access and edit each domain summary from its corresponding page in the assessment.

Accessing the AEPSi Curriculum Reference Guide

From the **CODRF Summary** page, there is a direct link to the relevant AEPSi Curriculum Reference Guide, which contains the curriculum content from either the *AEPS® Curriculum for Birth to Three Years* or *AEPS® Curriculum for Three to Six Years*.

Click the link or the associated image and a new browser window will appear. You can easily locate the intervention activities in the curriculum that correspond to specific goals and objectives identified with the AEPS Test.

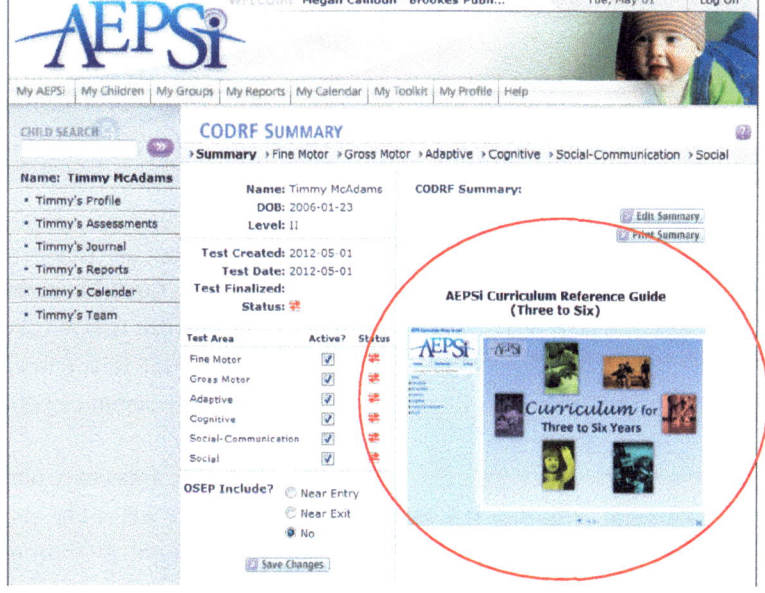

Selecting Test Areas

On the **CODRF Summary** page, you will see a list of the six domain areas with options to select or deselect one or more of the areas (up to 5). When you create a new CODRF, all six domain areas are activated by default. To deactivate or opt out of one or more areas, deselect the areas and click the *Save Changes* button. When an area has been deactivated, *n/a* will appear under the Status column. Only areas that are active will appear on the top navigation menu of the CODRF.

If you deselect a domain area that has previously entered data, the data will not disappear. You will no longer have access to the area and the data will not appear in reports, unless you reactivate the area.

If an assessment has already been flagged for OSEP Near Entry or Near Exit and you attempt to deactivate or opt out of one or more areas, you will be prevented from

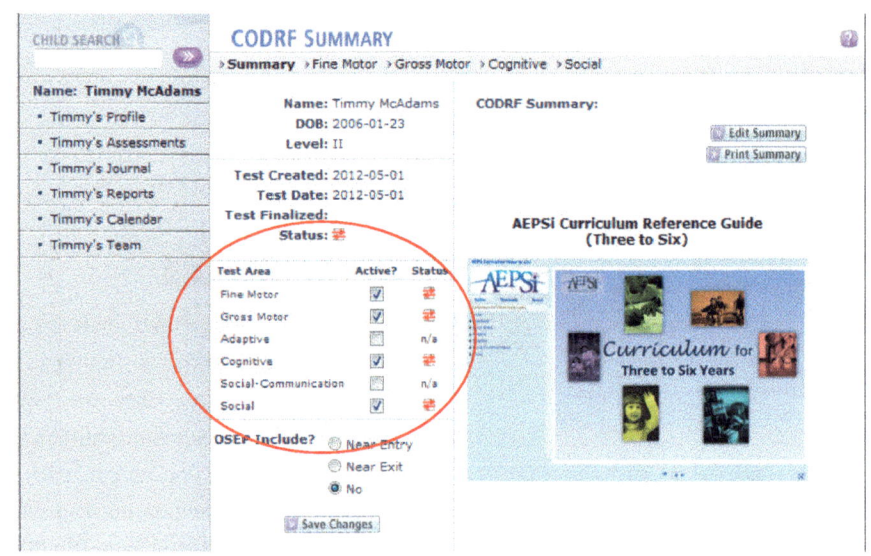

doing so. Similarly, if you have opted out of one or more of the areas, you will not be permitted to flag the assessment for either OSEP Near Entry or Near Exit.

> *Note: Opting out of one or more domain areas is only available for individual child assessments. This feature is not available for group assessments.*

OSEP Include

If the child has been flagged as an OSEP Participant in his or her child profile, an option will appear on the **CODRF Summary** page allowing you to include this assessment in OSEP near-entry or near-exit reporting. You may select either Near Entry, Near Exit, or No next to the OSEP Include? option.

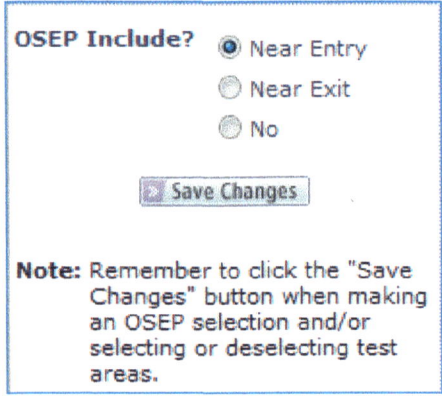

If the child is not an OSEP Participant, the OSEP Include? option will not appear on the **CODRF Summary** page. Flagging an assessment for Near Entry or Near Exit tells AEPSi which assessments to pull data from when running the OSEP Near Entry and Near Exit reports as well as the ECO Child Outcome Summary Form Ratings.

If one or more areas have not been selected for an assessment or opted out, you will not be able to select OSEP Near Entry or Near Exit for an assessment. An error message will appear, stating "OSEP cannot be selected because an area has been 'opted out.'" Likewise, if an assessment has already been flagged for OSEP Near Entry or Near Exit and you attempt to deselect or opt out of one or more areas, you will be prevented from doing so.

Filling in a CODRF

At the top of each domain page within an assessment, below the navigation bar, is the child's name, the domain, and the assessment level, as well as a button that allows you to view/edit that domain's summary and a button that allows you to print that area of the assessment, with or without the criteria.

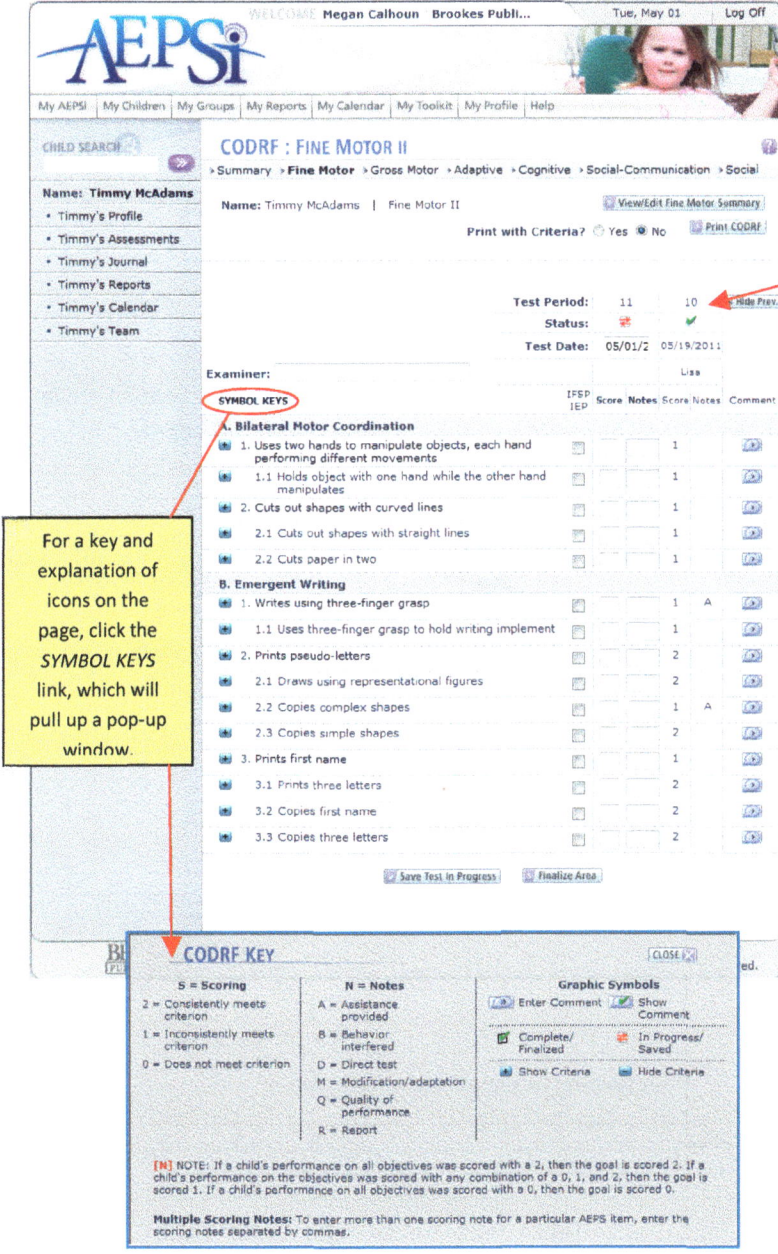

The remainder of each domain page consists of test information and the strands in this domain. The test information, including test period, CODRF status, test date, and examiner name, appears above the strands. By default, the previous CODRF information is shown in a second vertical column. You may hide the previous CODRF information by clicking the *Hide Prev.* button.

Prior to recording the CODRF results, please enter the test date and examiner's name.

Note: The test date should be the date the assessment was administered, not necessarily the date it was entered in AEPSi, and the examiner should be the person who administered the assessment, not necessarily the same person who is recording the results.

According to the guidelines for administering and scoring AEPS outlined in *AEPS® Administration Guide*, enter the corresponding numerical value in each *Score* box and the corresponding letter representing notes in the *Notes* box, and click the *IFSP/IEP* box accordingly for each item. To enter multiple scoring notes, enter each letter separated by a comma. The system will inform you if you have entered an invalid score/scoring note combination once you have clicked the *Finalize Area* button.

To view the criteria for an individual goal or objective, click the blue [+] icon to the left of the goal/objective.

Click the *View Curriculum* link at the end of each criterion to view the concurrent goals, environmental arrangements, intervention activities, etc. for the specific goal/objective. To hide the criteria, click the blue [-] icon.

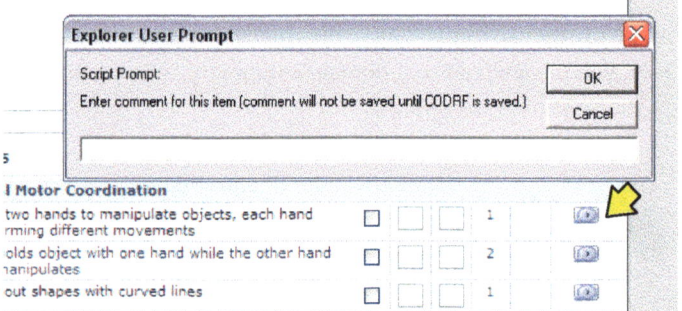

To enter a comment for a particular item, click the speech bubble icon to the far right of the item. A new window will pop up. Click inside the text box to type in your comments. Click the *OK* button to save the comment.

You may save your work on an area of the assessment at any time by clicking the *Save Test in Progress* button. Be sure you click this button before navigating to another page, or your work on that area will be lost.

If at any time you wish to finalize a domain, click the *Finalize Area* button at the bottom of the page. Once all active domains of an assessment have been finalized, the test will be considered finalized (the CODRF will appear complete, not in progress, in CODRF listings), and you will be able to run reports.

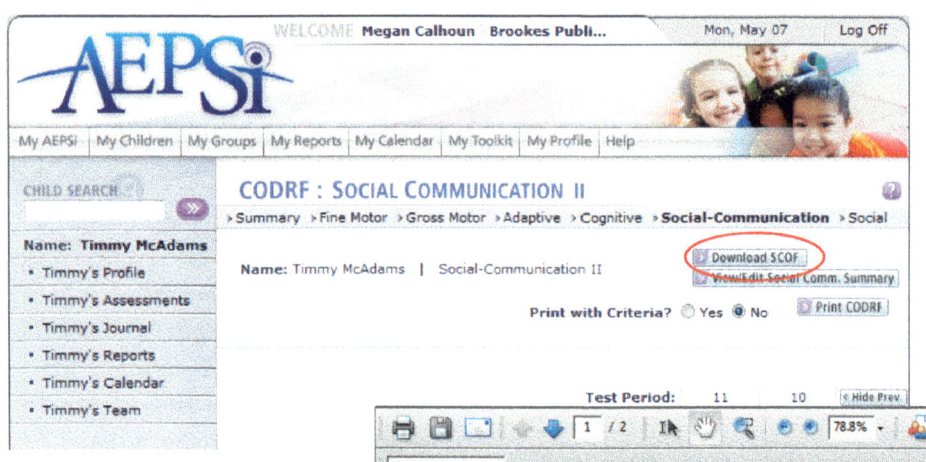

SCOF: Within the Social-Communication area, click *Download SCOF* to download the Social Communication Observation Form.

You may also access the SCOF download in the Download section of **My Toolkit.**

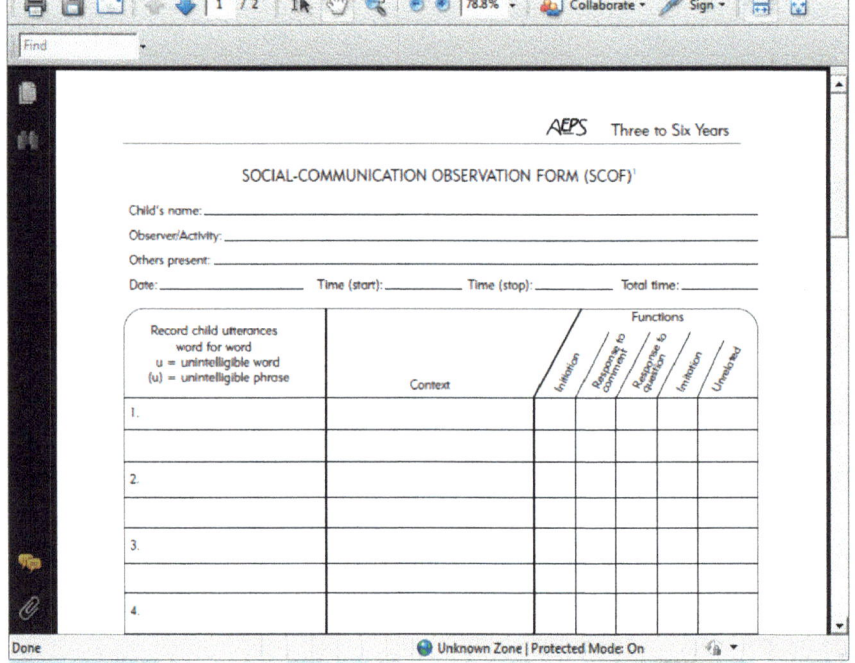

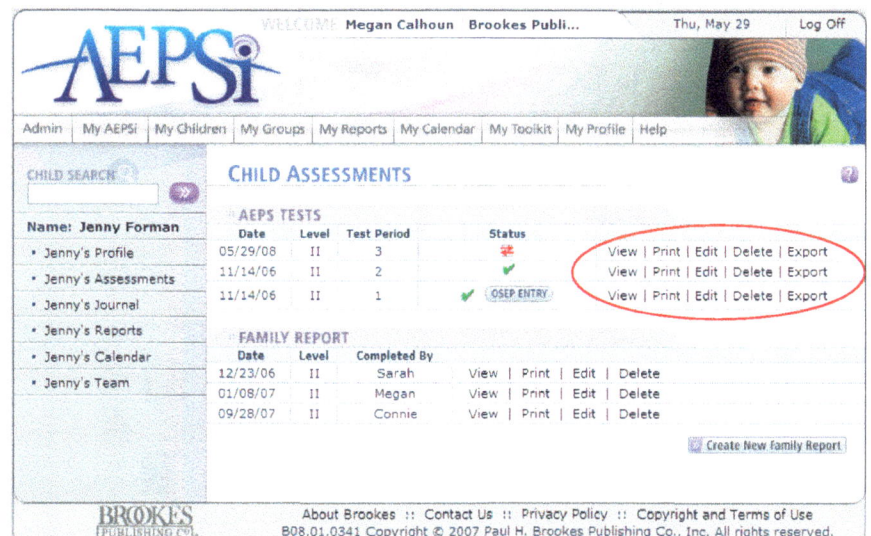

Viewing/Printing/ Editing/Deleting/ Exporting a CODRF

From the **Child Profile** or **Child Assessments** page, you may view, print, edit, delete, or export an assessment by clicking the corresponding link next to the assessment for which you would like to perform the action.

If you would like to include the criteria on a printed CODRF, use the *Print CODRF* button on the **CODRF Summary** page, selecting the print with criteria option. If you would like to just print one area of an assessment, go to the area of the assessment you would like to print and click on the *Print CODRF* button at the top of the page—you have the option of including the criteria or not.

Copy Scores from Previous Assessment

Once you have a completed CODRF for a child, you will have the ability to copy scores from that test when creating a new CODRF for the same child. When you click the *Create New CODRF* button, a pop-up box will appear presenting you with three options for copying over scores from the *previous* assessment:

1. Copy scores of 2 only with accompanying scoring notes
2. Copy all scores and scoring notes
3. Do not copy scores from previous AEPS Test

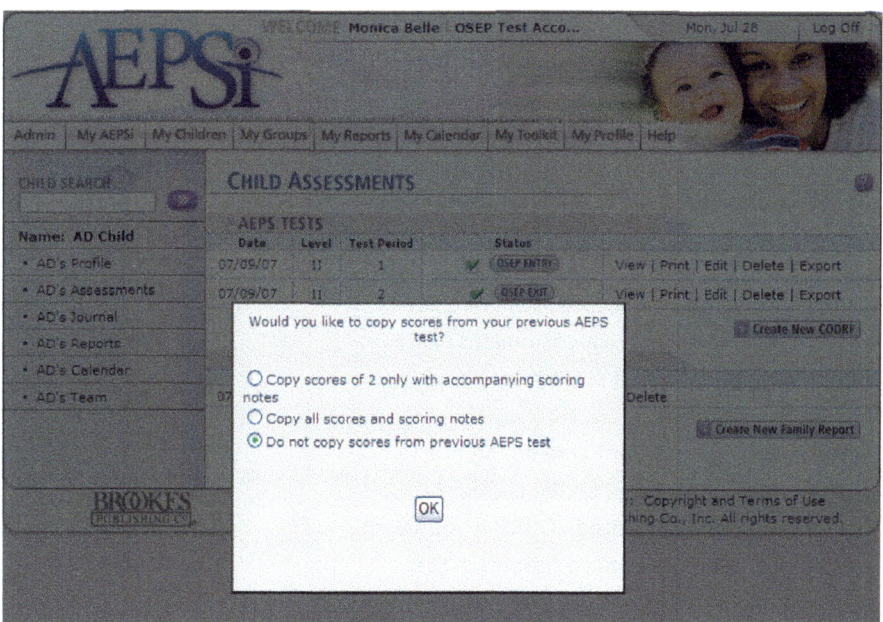

This is a time-saving measure that will prevent you from having to re-enter scores for a child that have not changed since the previous assessment period.

Note: The option for copying scores from a previous test will only appear if the previous test and current test are the same level.

AEPSi Provider Guide | 19

Customized CODRFs

At the bottom of the **CODRF Summary** page, there is a section where you can customize CODRFs. You may choose to customize a CODRF for any number of reasons.

For example, Timmy scored fairly high on his last AEPS assessment. On his next assessment, you'd like to assess only skills that have not yet emerged for Timmy. You can customize Timmy's new CODRF to show only the items on which he scored a 0 in his previous assessment.

Another example would be that you have already entered some assessment information for Timmy. You now want to create a customized CODRF based on items that have not yet been scored on his current CODRF.

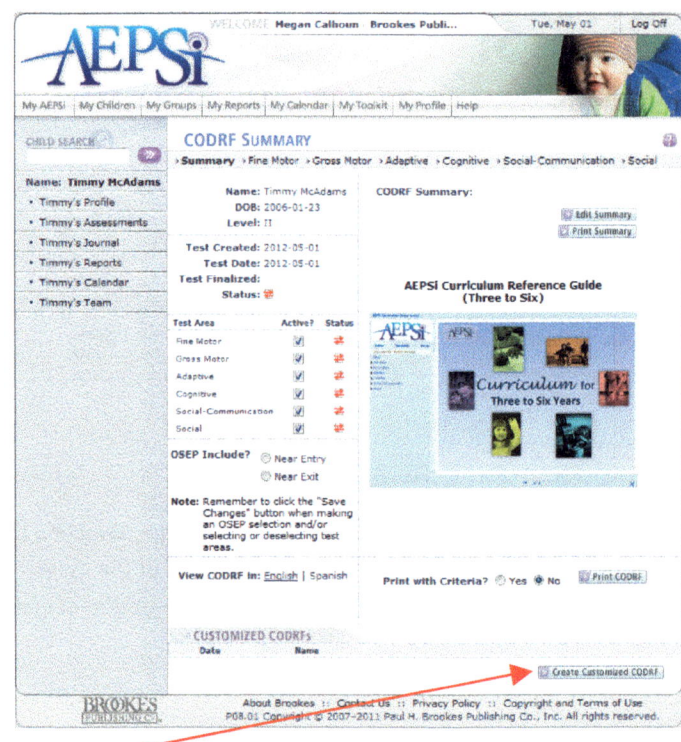

To customize a child's CODRF, click the *Create Customized CODRF* button to be taken to the **Create Customized CODRF** page. This page will allow you to create a custom CODRF based on the areas you want to assess, the child's previous scores, notes on the child's previous assessments, and previously indicated IFSP/IEP goals. You can also create the custom CODRF based on current scores, notes, and IFSP/IEP targets, as well as items that have not yet been scored.

To begin customizing a CODRF, select the areas you wish to include on your customized CODRF by checking the box next to each area's name.

Select whether you want to create the customized CODRF based on the current CODRF or the previously completed CODRF. If you select the current CODRF, you have the option to select items that have not yet been scored. Select the Yes checkbox to only include items that have not yet been scored.

Next, you can choose from three classifications of options that will narrow the scope of the customized CODRF.

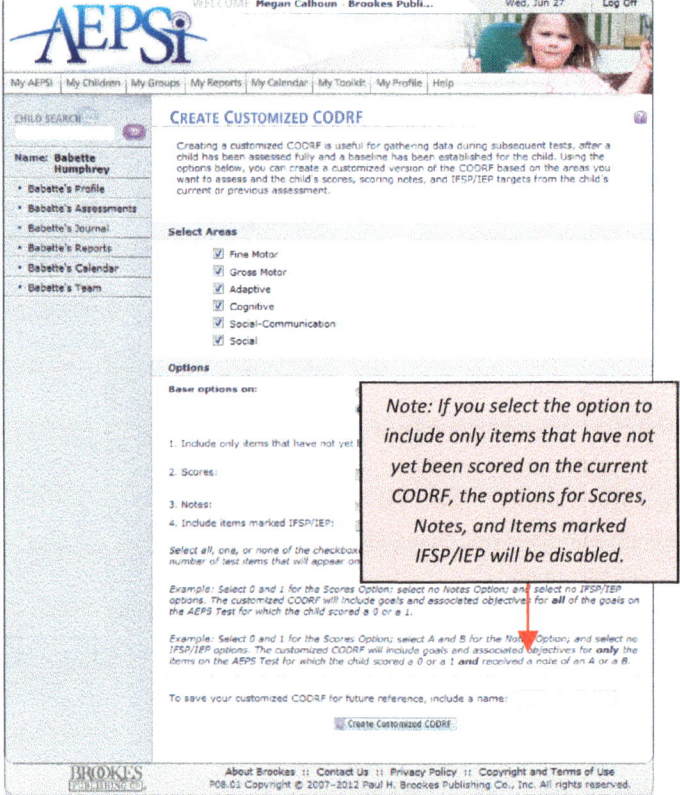

20 | AEPSi Provider Guide

Scores

Check the boxes next to the scores (0, 1, 2) to include those items on the customized CODRF. For example, to include only those items on which the child scored a 0, click the box next to the 0.

Notes

Check the boxes next to the notes (A, B, D, M, Q, R) to include only those items on the customized CODRF.

Include Items Marked IFSP/IEP

Click the Yes checkbox to include those items from the previous or current CODRF that are marked IFSP/IEP on the customized CODRF.

To save your customized CODRF, type in a name for future reference. When you have made your selections for the customized CODRF and named it, click the *Create Customized CODRF* button at the bottom of the page. A screen will pop up that shows your customized CODRF.

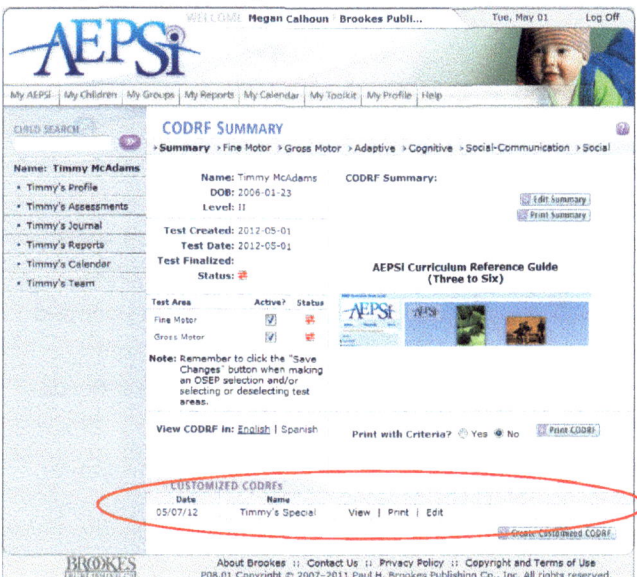

When you're ready to go back and enter in assessment data into a customized CODRF, go to the **CODRF Summary** page. You will see a list of all your customized CODRFs.

By clicking the *Edit* link, you will be taken to the customized CODRF where you will be able to enter in the assessment results. (Links that will allow you to view or print the customized CODRF will also be on the **CODRF Summary** page.)

Note: Any data that you enter into the customized CODRF form will populate the six areas of your current assessment. Once you have finished entering your data into the Customized CODRF, please remember to go to each assessment area and finalize.

Child Outcomes Summary Form (COSF)

If you have near-entry assessment data from another assessment tool(s) and the assessment tool provides ECO ratings for the three outcomes, you can create a Child Outcomes Summary Form within AEPSi. The Child Outcomes Summary Form will replace the AEPSi near-entry assessment. AEPSi will automatically transform the ECO ratings into the equivalent AEPS OSEP raw scores and you will be able to run all OSEP near-entry data reports.

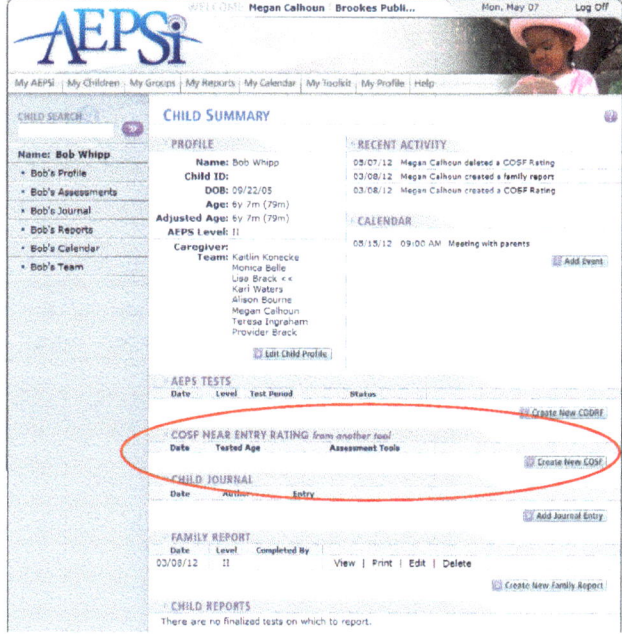

Note: You should use the COSF ONLY if another assessment tool was used to assess a child at OSEP near entry. The COSF form is not available for near exit data.

Create Child Outcomes Summary Form

The Child Outcomes Summary Form (COSF) option will appear on the **Child Summary** page only if the child has been marked for OSEP inclusion on his or her profile page and an AEPS Assessment has not been created or marked for Near Entry.

To create a COSF, first click the *Create New COSF* button under the **COSF Near Entry Rating from another assessment tool** tab on the **Child Summary** page.

Enter the date of the assessment.

Enter a description of assessment tools used to determine the entry COSF rating.

Enter a COSF rating between 1 and 7 for the three Child Outcomes: Positive Social-Emotional Skills, Acquisition and Use of Knowledge and Skills, and Appropriate Behaviors to Meet Needs.

For each of the three outcomes, enter supporting evidence/notes in the text area field.

Click the *Save* button.

View/Print/Edit/Delete Child Outcomes Summary Form

You may view, print, edit, or delete an existing completed COSF form by clicking the appropriate link from the **Child Summary** page.

Family Report

Section 10

The Family Report is an important part of the AEPS assessment because even teachers, school specialists, and home visitors don't get the chance to observe a child in every environment. The Family Report can be sent home for the family member or caregiver to fill out and return to you. Once the report is completed, you may enter it into AEPSi.

Entering a New Family Report

To enter a new Family Report, click the *Create New Family Report* button from the **Child Summary**, **Child Assessments**, or **Child Reports** pages.

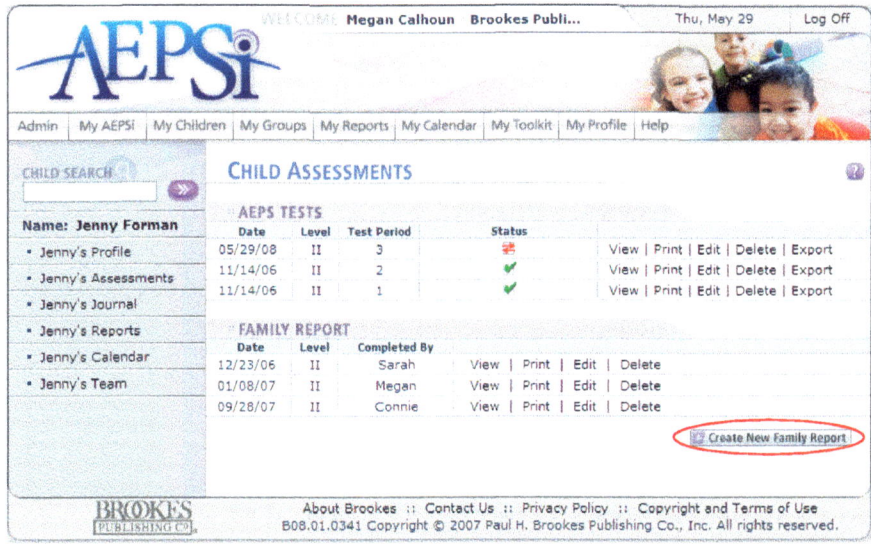

For each Family Report, enter the following information that will comprise the Family Report Summary, and click *Save*:

- Who completed the report
- A short report summary

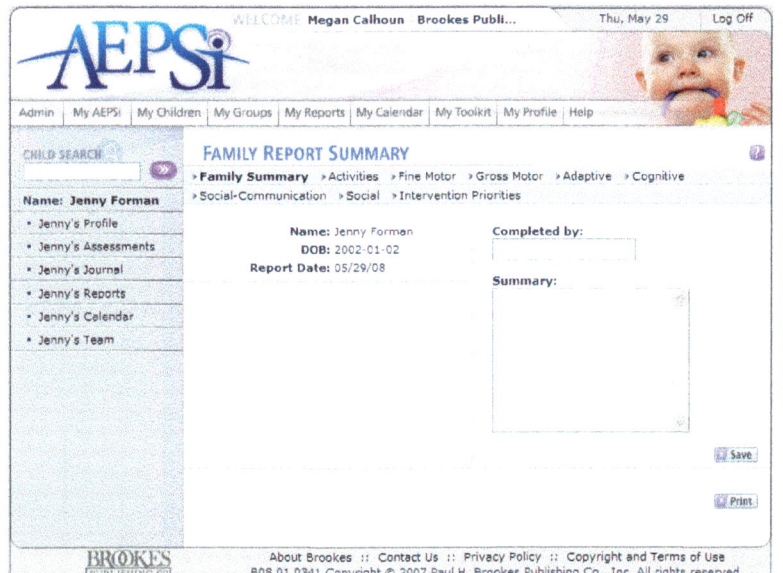

> *Note: It is recommended that within the report summary you include the following items:*
> - *The date the family or caregiver(s) completed the report*
> - *The child's siblings and their ages*
> - *The name of the family member(s)/caregiver(s) who completed the form*

Sections of the Family Report

Links to each section of the Family Report are on the top of all **Family Report** pages: *Family Summary, Activities, Fine Motor, Gross Motor, Adaptive, Cognitive, Social-Communication, Social,* and *Intervention Priorities.* To go to a specific section of the Family Report, click the named link.

Activities

- Enter the date reviewed with family.
- Answer the questions by typing the answers into each text box provided.
- Click the *Save* button.

Fine Motor, Gross Motor, Adaptive, Social-Communication, and Social

- Enter the date reviewed with family.
- Enter the scores in the boxes under the SCORE column.
- Answer the question(s) by typing the answer(s) into each text box provided.
- Click the *Save* button.

Cognitive

- Enter the date reviewed with family.
- Enter the scores in the boxes under the SCORE column.
- Click on the check boxes to select as many answers as possible.
- Answer the question(s) by typing the answer(s) into each text box provided.
- Click the *Save* button.

> *Note: Please be sure to check off the appropriate information in a two-part question that requires additional answers to score a "Y." AEPSi will not automatically catch this for you (e.g., for the question: "Does your child understand and say opposite words?" you must also select a minimum number of word pairs in order to score a "Y." Please make sure that you check off these word pairs if you enter a "Y.")*

Intervention Priorities

- Enter the date reviewed with family.
- List the parent(s)'/caregiver(s)' most important priorities by typing them into each numbered text box.
- Click the *Save* button.

Viewing/Printing/Editing/Deleting a Family Report

To view, print, edit, or delete a Family Report, click the corresponding link in the Family Report portion of the **Child Summary, Child Assessments,** or **Child Reports** pages next to the Family Report on which you would like to perform that action.

FAMILY REPORT

Date	Level	Completed By				
04/11/12	II	Henry	View	Print	Edit	Delete
12/20/10	II	Megan	View	Print	Edit	Delete
03/08/12	II		View	Print	Edit	Delete

» Create New Family Report

Child Reports

Section 11

Once you have a finalized assessment for a child, you will be able to run individual Child Reports through either the Child Reports potion of the **Child Summary** page or by selecting the **Child Reports** page from the left navigation bar (e.g., *Timmy's Reports*).

You will have the option to view, print, or export seven types of reports: Score Summary, Graphed Scores, Child Progress Record, Provider Notes, IFSP/IEP Summary, Eligibility Cutoff Scores, and Present Level of Functioning.

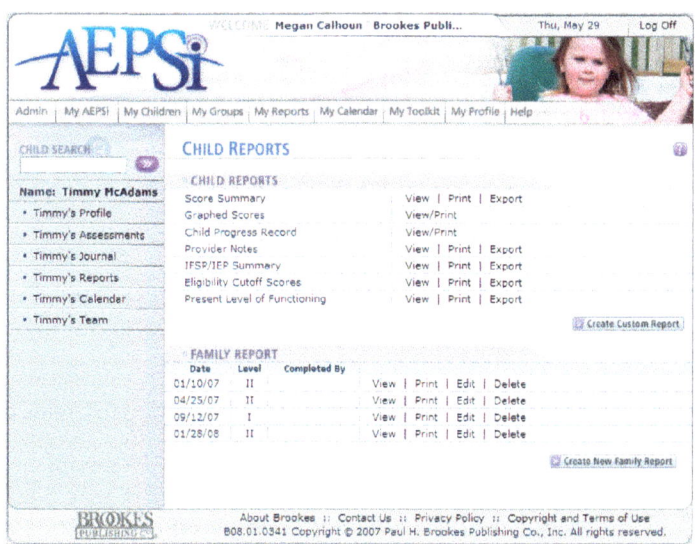

Score Summary

The Score Summary report shows test date, raw score, raw score possible, and percent score for each area of the CODRF for up to the last four CODRFs entered.

To run a Score Summary report, click the *View* or *Print* link. You will be directed to a page that shows the range of test periods. Select the button next to the range of test periods on which you want to run the report, and click the *Create Report* button. The Score Summary report will appear in a new browser window.

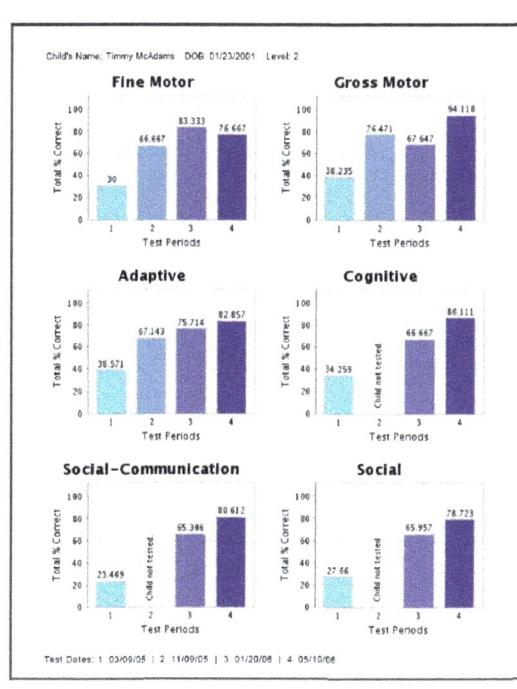

Graphed Scores

Graphed Scores show bar graphs that represent CODRF scores for different test periods. By comparing test periods as side-by-side bar graphs, you have a quick visible representation of a child's progress over time.

The following reporting options are available:

<u>% of Mastered and Emerging (2 and 1)</u>: This report will add all items that were scored 1's and 2's and display as a percentage of the total score possible for each area.

AEPSi Provider Guide | 25

% of Mastered (2): This report will add all items that were scored 2's and display as a percentage of the total score possible for each area.

% of Emerging (1): This report will add all items that were scored 1's and display as a percentage of the total score possible for each area.

% of Scoring Note A: This report shows the percentage of items that had an accompanying scoring note of A for each area.

% of Scoring Note B: This report shows the percentage of items that had an accompanying scoring note of B for each area.

% of Scoring Note M: This report shows the percentage of items that had an accompanying scoring note of M for each area.

% of Scoring Note Q: This report shows the percentage of items that had an accompanying scoring note of Q for each area.

% of Scoring Note R: This report shows the percentage of items that had an accompanying scoring note of R for each area.

Child Progress Record

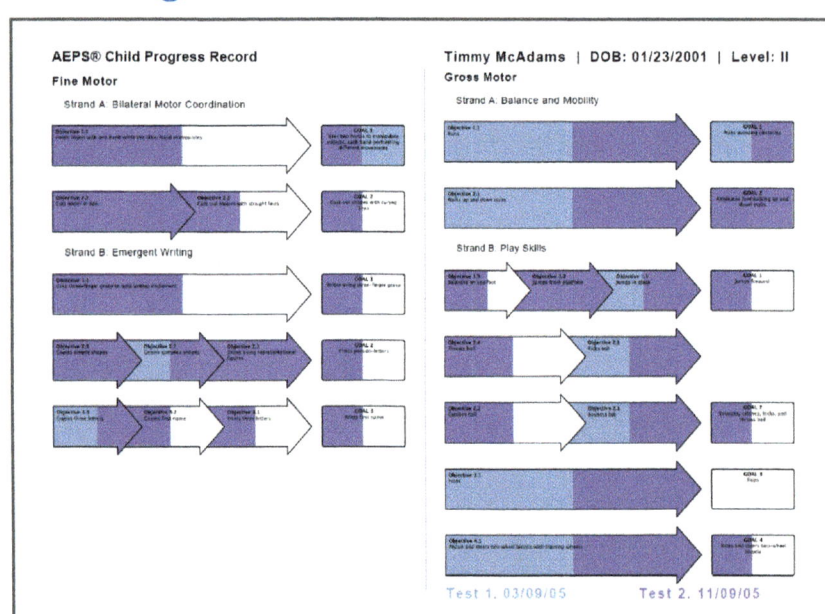

A Child Progress Record helps family members and caregivers participate in the ongoing monitoring of their child's progress. The Child Progress Record is a visual representation of a child's accomplishments, current targets, and future goals and objectives. As a child meets the standard criteria for a goal or objective, shading indicates the child's progress.

To view or print a Child Progress Record, click the *View/Print* link. You will be directed to a page that shows the available test periods for the child. Select up to two test periods to include in the Child Progress Record. Once you've selected the test period(s), click the *Create Report* button, and a PDF file of the Child Progress Record will open in a new window with options to print or save it to your computer.

Note: Make sure Adobe Acrobat Reader is installed on your computer or you will be unable to view or print the Graphed Scores report or a Child Progress Record.

Provider Notes

The Provider Notes report shows all of the items in an assessment that were marked with a note (A, B, D, M, Q, R) and any corresponding scores and comments for those items.

To view Provider Notes, click the *View* link. To print Provider Notes, click the *Print* link. You will be directed to a page that shows the available test periods for the child. Select one test period and click the *Create Report* button. The Provider Notes report will appear in a new browser window.

IFSP/IEP Summary

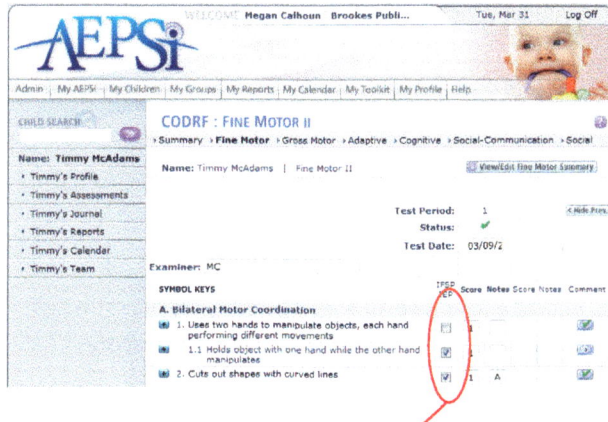

The IFSP/IEP Summary shows all items that had the IFSP/IEP box checked on an assessment. This report can be used to help write goals for a child's IFSP or IEP. The report also includes sample IFSP/IEP goals.

To run an IFSP/IEP Summary, click the *View* or *Print* link. You will be directed to a page that shows the available test periods for the child. Select one test period and click the *Create Report* button. The IFSP/IEP Summary will appear in a new browser window.

Eligibility Cutoff Scores

The Eligibility Cutoff Scores Report shows the Area Goal Score and the Cutoff Score for each area of an assessment and then tells whether the child falls within the range for typically developing children or is at or below the range for typically developing children.

For more information about the eligibility cutoff scores, see the "Using AEPS® to Determine Eligibility for IDEA Services" document in the Documents and Downloads section of **My Toolkit**.

To run Eligibility Cutoff Scores, click the *View* or *Print* link. You will be directed to a page that shows the available test periods for the child. Select one test period and click the *Create Report* button. The Eligibility Cutoff Scores will appear in a new browser window.

Present Level of Functioning

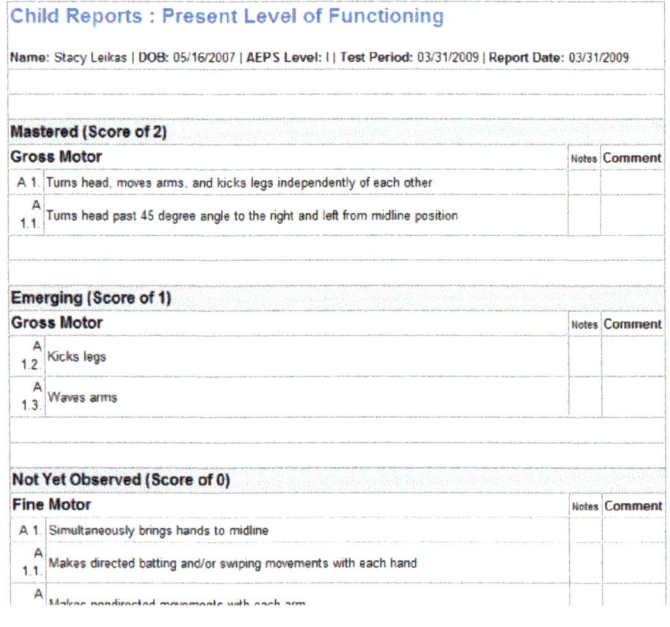

The Present Level of Functioning report shows all items from an assessment grouped by score: Mastered (2), Emerging (1), and Not Yet Observed (0).

To run Present Level of Functioning, click the *View* or *Print* link. You will be directed to a page that shows the available test periods for the child. Select one test period and click the *Create Report* button. The Present Level of Functioning report will appear in a new browser window.

Running Reports in Spanish

Any Child Report that includes the pertinent items from the AEPSi assessment (Child Progress Record, Provider Notes, IFSP/IEP Summary, and Present Level of Functioning) can be run so that those items appear in Spanish on the report.

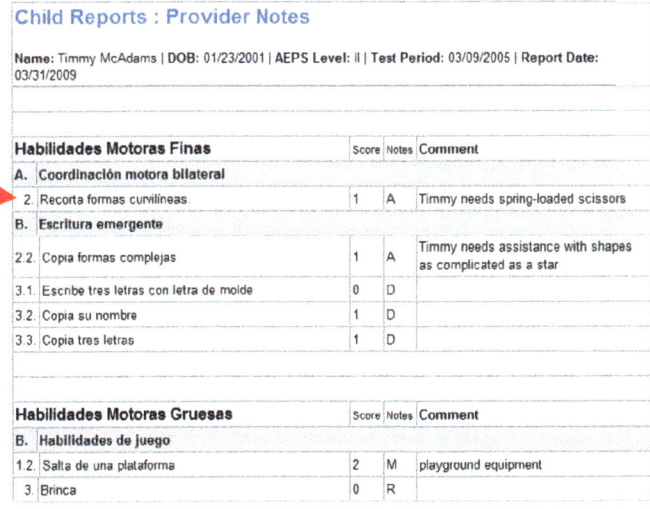

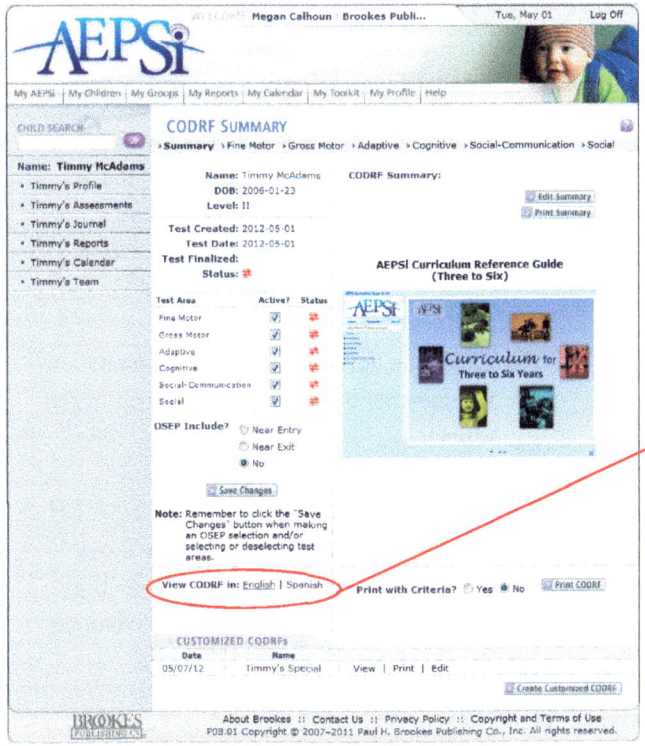

To do this, you just need to make sure that the assessment on which you want to run the report is marked for Spanish on that assessment's **CODRF Summary** Page.

Create Custom Child Report

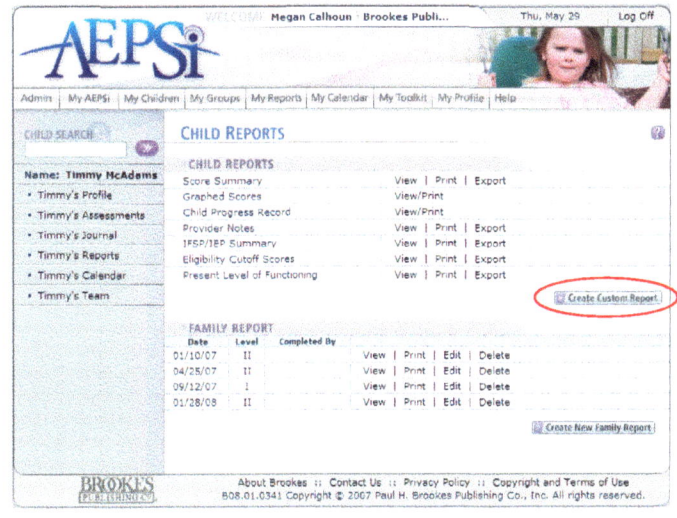

The Custom Child Report enables you to make a customized report on any of a child's finalized assessments based on assessment areas, scores, notes, and indicated IFSP/IEP goals.

To create a Custom Child Report, click the *Create Custom Report* button on the **Child Reports** page below the Child Reports section.

You will be directed to the **Child Reports: Create Custom** page.

Select the test period on which you would like to create the custom report.

To begin customizing a report, select which assessment areas you would like to include in the report.

AEPSi Provider Guide | 29

Next, you can choose from three options that will narrow the scope of the customized report (Scores, Notes, Include items marked IFSP/IEP). Next to each option is a list of check boxes.

Check as many boxes as you would like to apply to the new report.

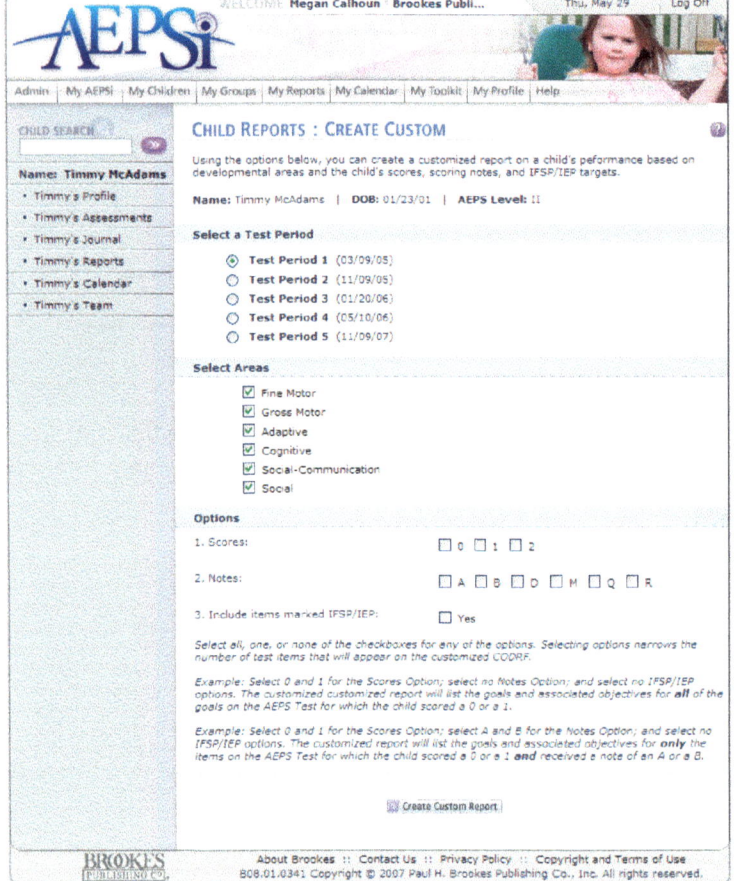

Scores
Check the boxes next to the score(s) to include only those items in the customized report.

For example, to include only those items on which the child scored a 0, check the box next to the 0. To include only those questions on which the child scored a 1 or 2, check the boxes next to the 1 or 2.

Notes
Check the boxes next to the note(s) to include only those items in the customized report.

Include Items Marked IFSP/IEP
Check the Yes box to include only those items that were marked IFSP/IEP on the finalized CODRF on which you are running the customized report.

When you have made your selections for the customized report, click the *Create Customized Report* button at the bottom of the page. A screen will pop up that shows your customized report. See **Section 14: My Reports** for more information.

My Groups

Section 12

The **My Groups** section is where you can create AEPS assessment activities. AEPS assessment activities enable you to complete the entire AEPS Test in either home- or center-based settings with just 7 or 8 activities.

The **My Groups** main page is where you can create group assessments and journal entries. It lists previously entered group assessments that are in progress and includes the date, group name, child names, AEPS level (Level I: Birth to 3 years; Level II: 3–6 years), and assessment type (Center-Based, Routine Activity, or Standard CODRF).

It also lists previously entered group journal entries that are in progress and includes date, author, group name, child(ren) name(s), and the first few words of the entry.

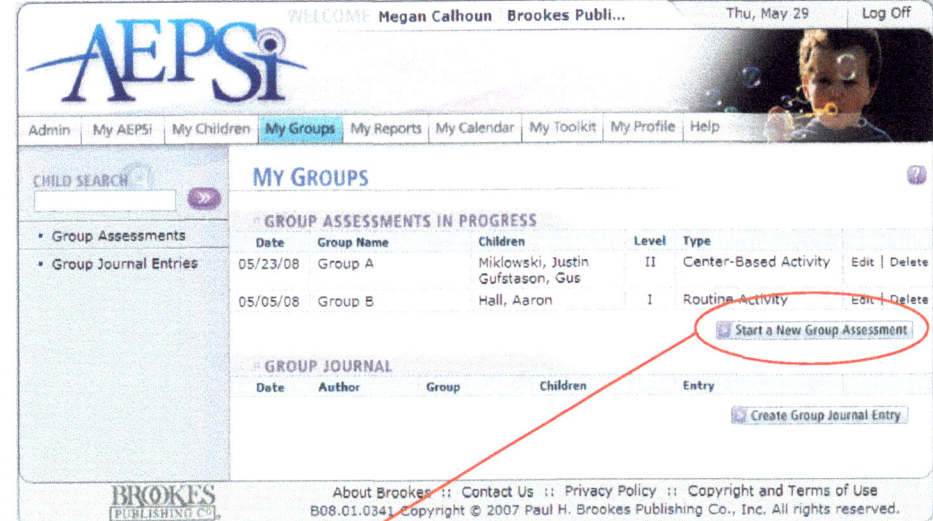

Creating a Group

To start a new group assessment, click the *Start a New Group Assessment* button below the list of assessments in progress.

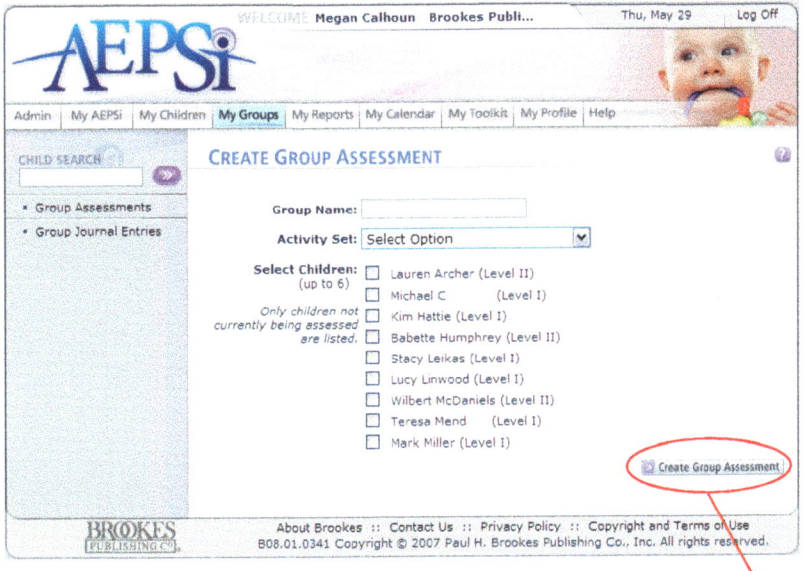

Note: Group Assessments can be done with just 1 child if you want to assess the child with an activity assessment.

You will be taken to the **Create Group Assessment** page. On this page, first enter a name for the group assessment you are creating, then select the type of assessment you would like to give this group:

- Routine Activity Set (Level I)
- Center-Based Activity Set (Level I or Level II)
- a Standard CODRF (Level I or Level II)

Next, select up to 6 of your children (all of the same Level) to participate in the group assessment by clicking the check boxes next to their names.

Finally, click the *Create Group Assessment* button.

Group Assessment Summary

You will be taken to the **Group CODRF Summary** page after you create your group.

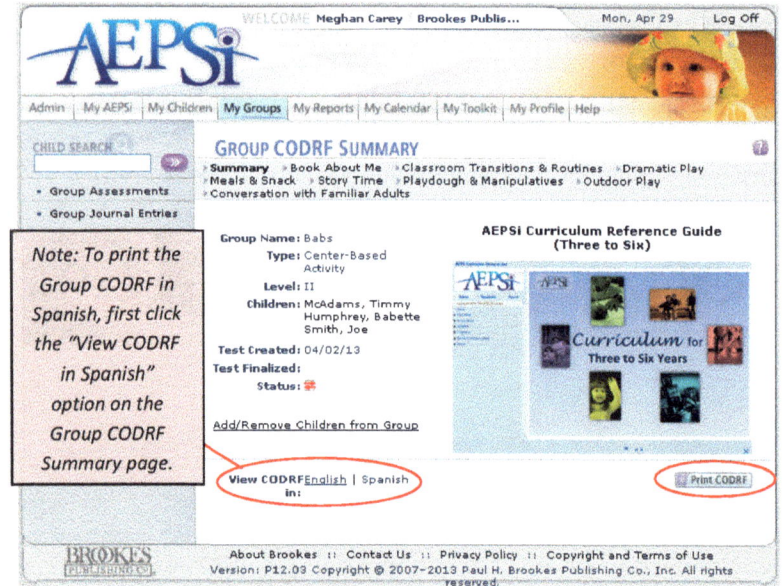

Note: To print the Group CODRF in Spanish, first click the "View CODRF in Spanish" option on the Group CODRF Summary page.

From here, you may print out the group assessment by selecting the *Print CODRF* button.

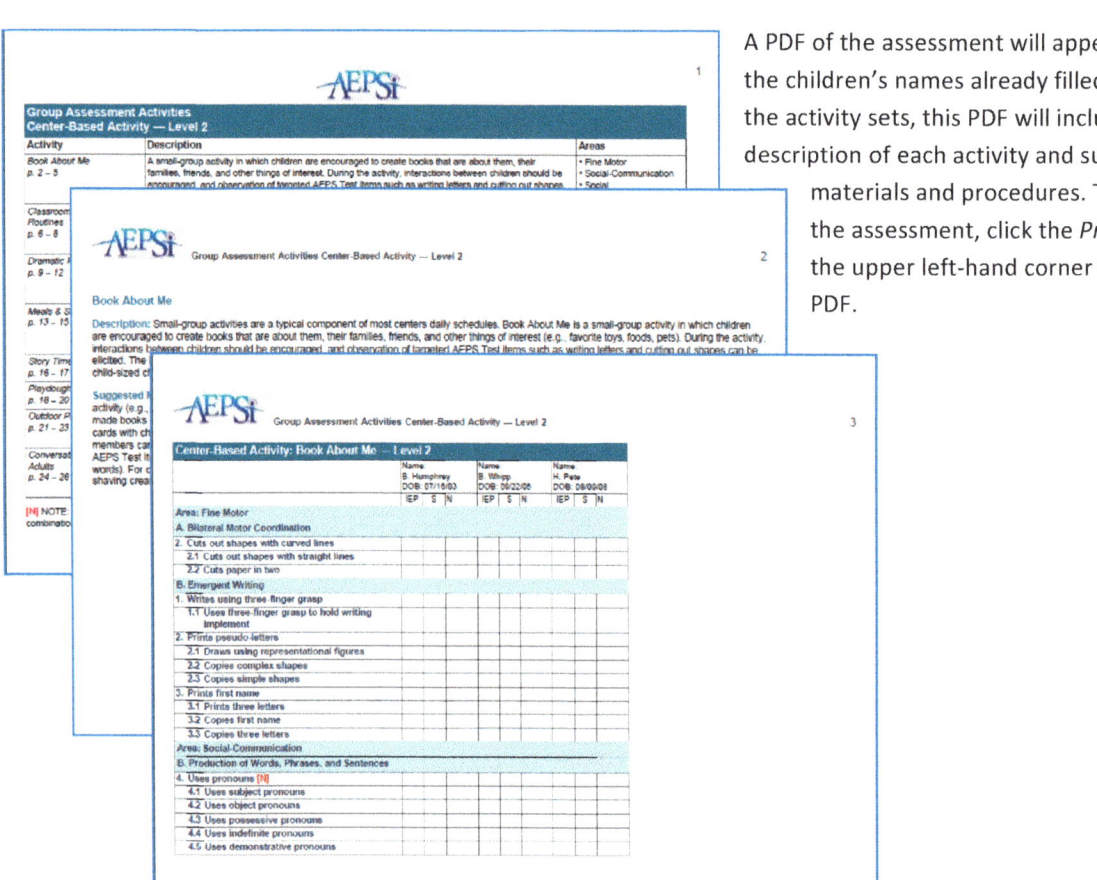

A PDF of the assessment will appear with the children's names already filled in. For the activity sets, this PDF will include a description of each activity and suggested materials and procedures. To print the assessment, click the *Print* icon in the upper left-hand corner of the PDF.

To enter the results of a group assessment, select the links at the top of the **Group CODRF Summary** page to go to a certain part of the assessment. You will then be able to fill in IFSP/IEP information, scores, and notes for each child.

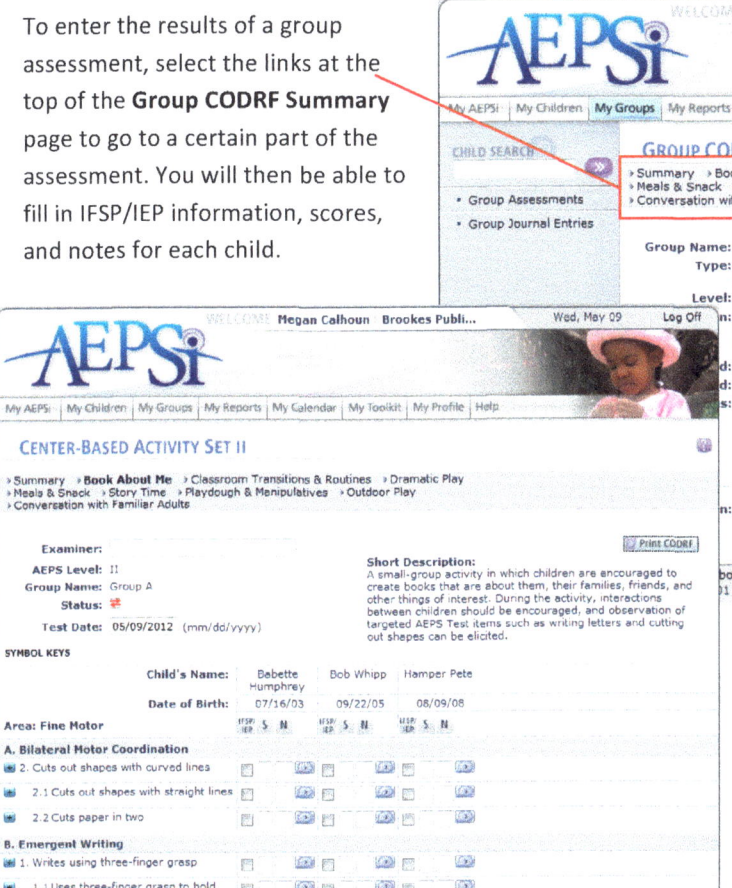

There is also a link to the AEPSi Curriculum Reference Guide on the **Group CODRF Summary** page. Click the link or the associated image and a new browser window will appear. The AEPSi Curriculum Reference Guide contains the curriculum content from either the *AEPS® Curriculum for Birth to Three Years* or *AEPS® Curriculum for Three to Six Years*. You can easily locate the intervention activities in the curriculum that correspond to specific goals and objectives identified with the test.

Editing a Group Assessment

To edit a group assessment that is in progress, click the *Edit* link beside the entry on the **My Groups** main page, or select the *Edit* link next to that group assessment from any of the **Child Summary** or **Child Assessment** pages of the children who are participating in that group assessment.

AEPSi Provider Guide | 33

Deleting a Group

Once you have entered all of the data for your group and finalized each activity or area, you must delete your group in order to automatically populate individual CODRFs for each child. To delete a group, go to the **My Groups** main page. Click the *Delete* link next to the group you want deleted. You can access an individual CODRF for a child by going to his or her **Child Summary** page.

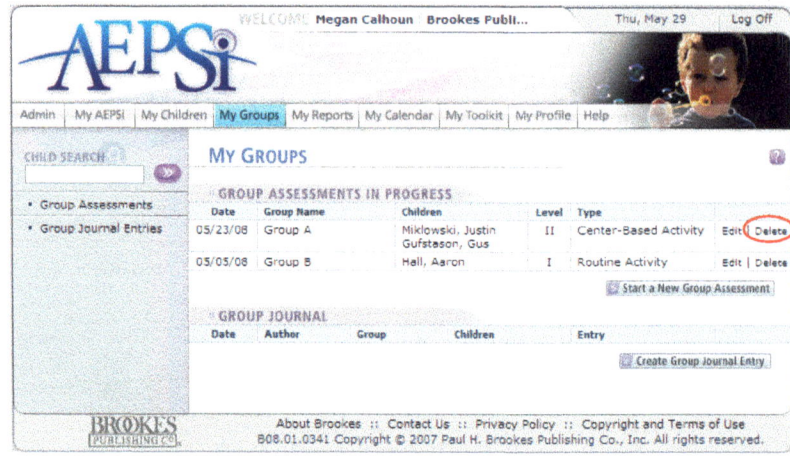

Note: You also have the ability to complete just some of the activities from a group activity set and then delete the group, allowing you to finish the assessment for each individual child who was in the group in the standard CODRF format.

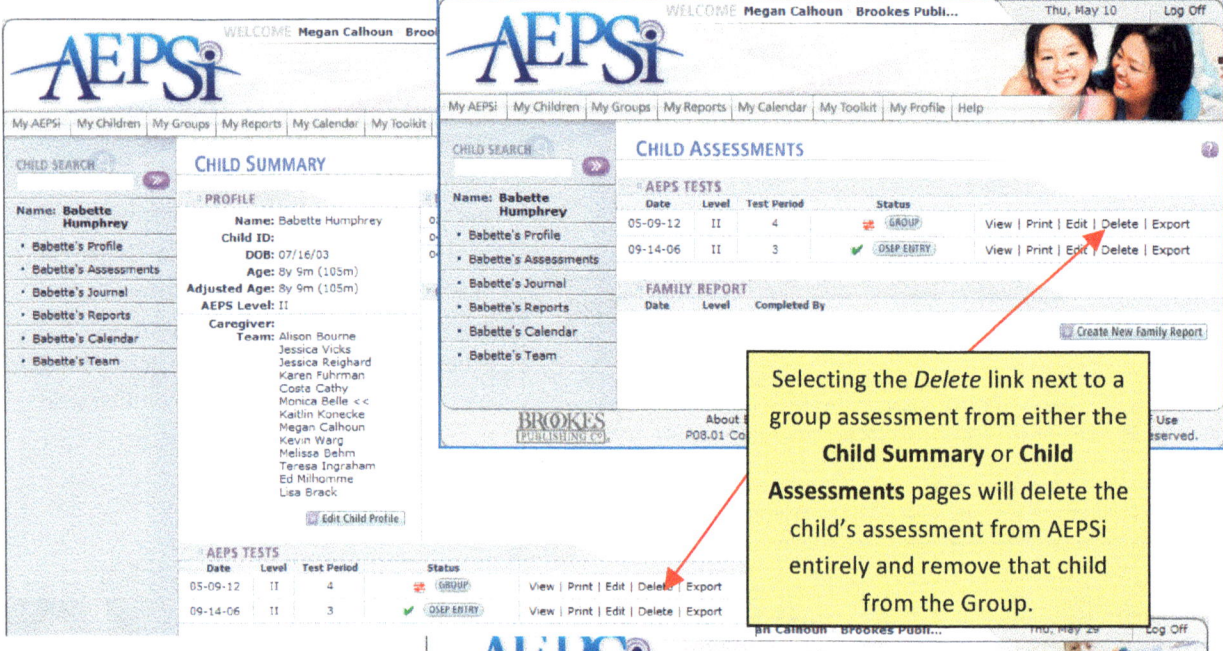

Selecting the *Delete* link next to a group assessment from either the **Child Summary** or **Child Assessments** pages will delete the child's assessment from AEPSi entirely and remove that child from the Group.

Creating a Group Journal Entry

To create a group journal entry, click the *Create New Group Journal Entry* button below the list of group journals in progress.

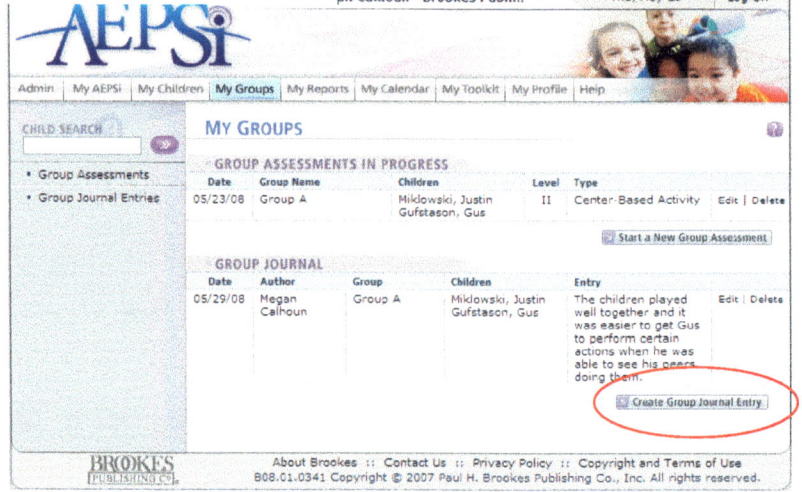

34 | AEPSi Provider Guide

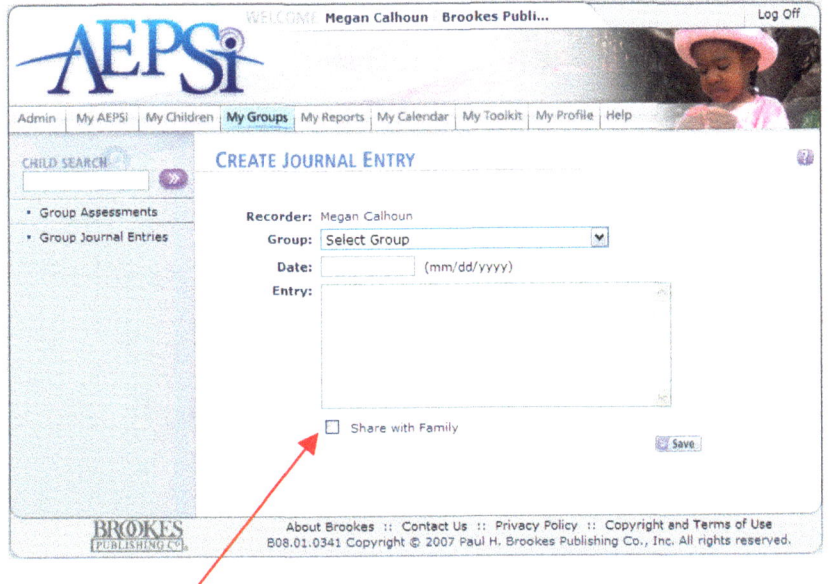

You will be taken to a page called **Create Journal Entry**.

Next to Group, select the group for which you would like to make a journal entry from the dropdown menu.

Enter in the date that the entry is made by clicking in the text box next to the Date field.

Enter your text in the Entry field.

Click *Share with Family* if you would like the family to be allowed to see the journal entry.

Click the *Save* button to save the journal entry.

Editing/Deleting a Group Journal Entry

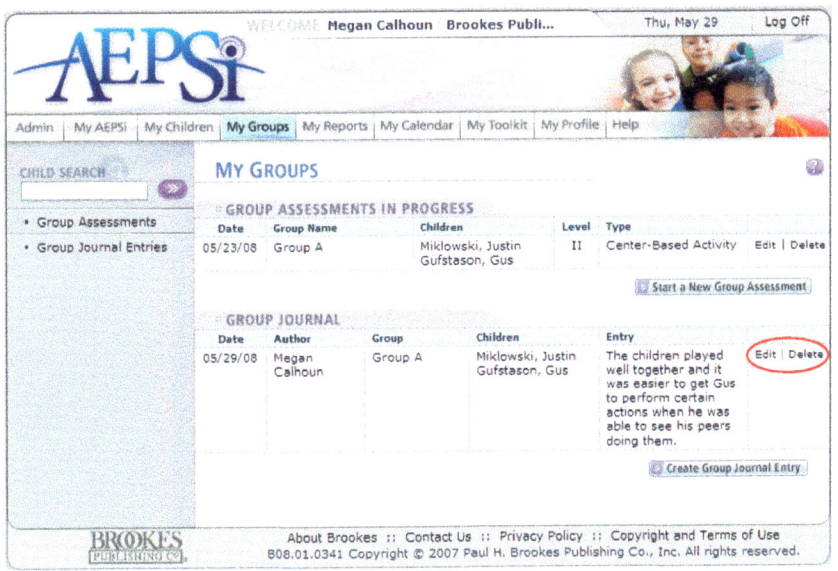

To edit a group journal entry that is in progress, click the *Edit* link beside the entry on the **My Groups** main page.

To delete a group journal entry that is in progress, click the *Delete* link beside the entry on the **My Groups** main page.

My Calendar

Section 13

The **My Calendar** page, accessed by clicking the **My Calendar** tab at the top of the screen, shows you a list of all upcoming events for which you have been marked as an attendee.

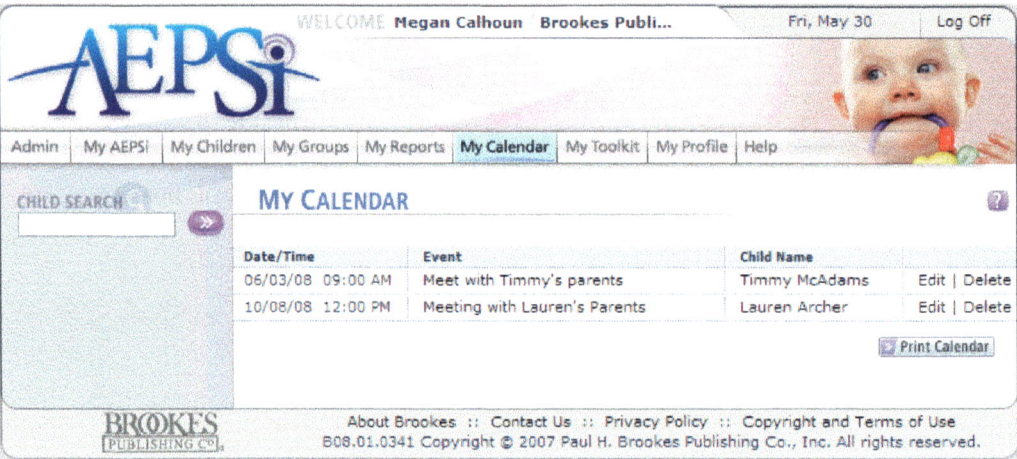

View an event by clicking the date/time or the description of the event you would like to view.

To delete an event, click *Delete* next to the event you'd like to delete. You will be asked if you are sure you want to delete this event. Click *OK* to continue deleting the event. Click *Cancel* if you do not wish to delete the event.

Edit an event by clicking *Edit* next to the event you'd like to edit. You will be taken to the **Child Calendar** page for that event. Make any needed changes and click the *Save* button.

Because all events must be tied to specific children in AEPSi, you can only add events from the **Child Summary** or **Child Calendar** pages.

To add an event, click the *Add Event* button on either the **Child Summary** or **Child Calendar** pages for the child whom you would like to schedule an event. You will be taken to a page where you will be prompted to enter the event date, event time, text about the event itself, and attendees. If you select yourself as an attendee, this event will appear on your **My Calendar** page.

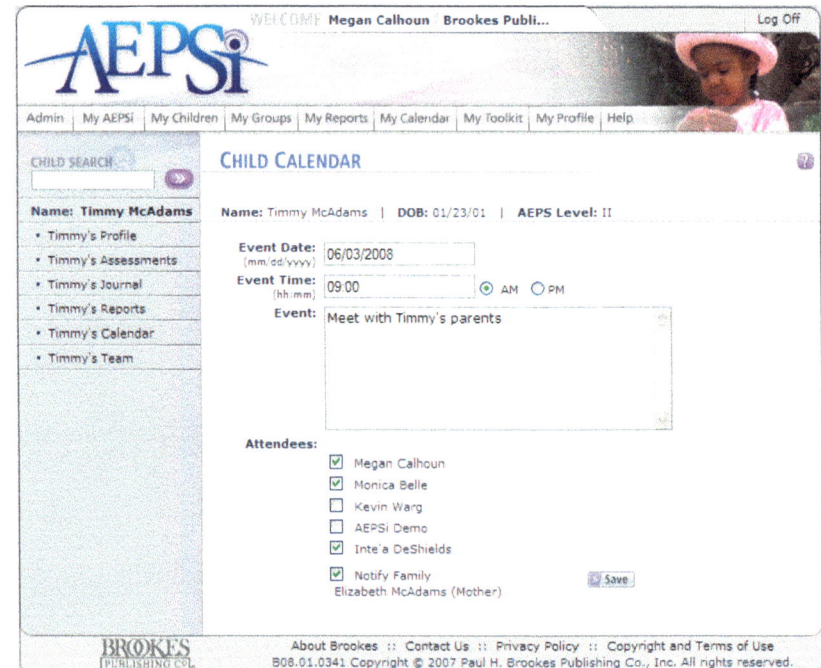

36 | AEPSi Provider Guide

My Reports

Section 14

AEPSi features powerful functions that make it easy to record, score, and track the AEPS Test and also enables you to quickly generate reports showing the status or progress over time for an individual child and groups of children. AEPSi generates the paperwork for reports that otherwise you would have to create by hand: Score Summary, Graphed Scores, IFSP/IEP Summary, Child Progress Record, and Present Level of Functioning Report for use at IFSP/IEP meetings.

You can also use AEPSi to turn AEPS Test scores into OSEP Child Outcomes reports with a single click. Your OSEP reports are reliable and valid and exportable into any format your state requires. In addition, you can compare a child's AEPS Test scores with rigorously researched cutoff scores to determine or corroborate the child's eligibility for services in most state systems. In addition to creating individual Child, Class, and Program Reports, programs in the same district, region, or state can be linked so that administrators can generate "roll-up" status and progress reports.

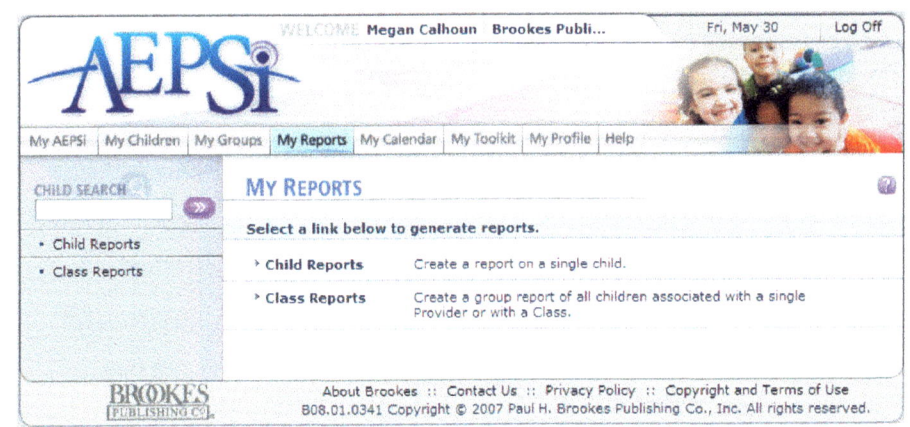

This section describes how to create individual reports for children, as well as Class Reports, and provides more detail on OSEP reporting and Eligibility Reports.

The **My Reports** section of AEPSi, accessed by clicking the **My Reports** tab at the top of the screen, allows you to access both Child and Class Reports. If you are also an AEPSi Administrator, there will be an additional link to Program Reports. For more information on Program Reports, please see the Administrator User Manual found in the **Admin** section of AEPSi under **Help** or by clicking the purple question mark buttons in the **Admin** section.

Child Reports

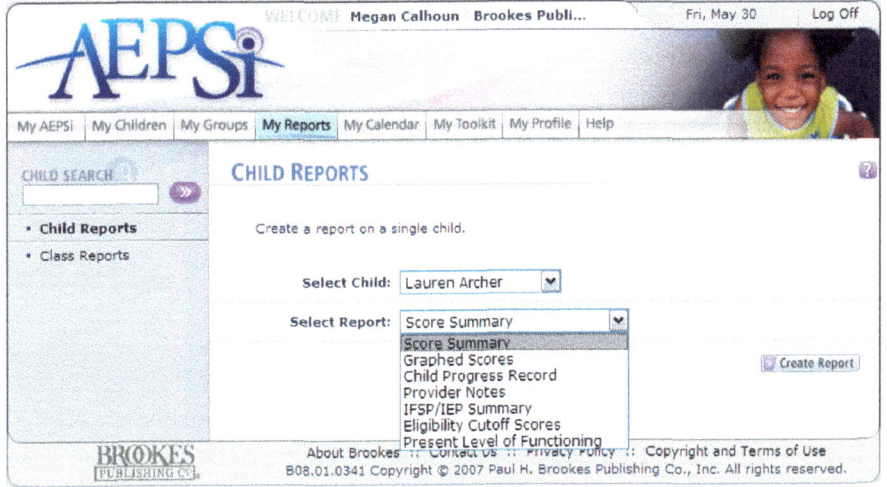

Providers and Administrators as well as Reviewers with access to child identifiable data may access Child Reports. As a Provider, you can only create Child Reports for children to whom you are assigned. Administrators and Reviewers with access to child identifiable data can view all Child Reports.

To run a Child Report from the **My Reports** section, select the name of the child on whom you'd like to run the report and then select the report you'd like to run for that child. To learn more about the individual Child Reports see *Section 11: Child Reports*.

Aggregate Reports

In addition to the individual Child Reports, you can create Aggregate Reports on the children to whom you are assigned.

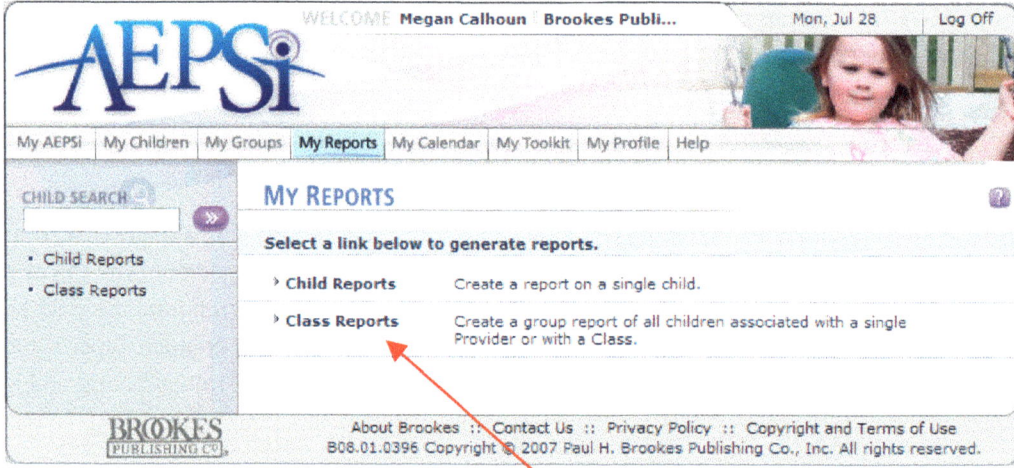

You can access these Aggregate Reports by clicking the *Class Reports* link on your **My Reports** page.

Class Reports

You can create group reports for all children who are assigned to you or who are assigned to one of your classes. The reports available include Group Snapshots that provide details on the assessment status of children as well as six OSEP reports.

You can run three types of aggregate reports in AEPSi:

- Group Snapshot Reports
- OSEP Categories Reports
- ECO Child Outcomes Summary Form Ratings

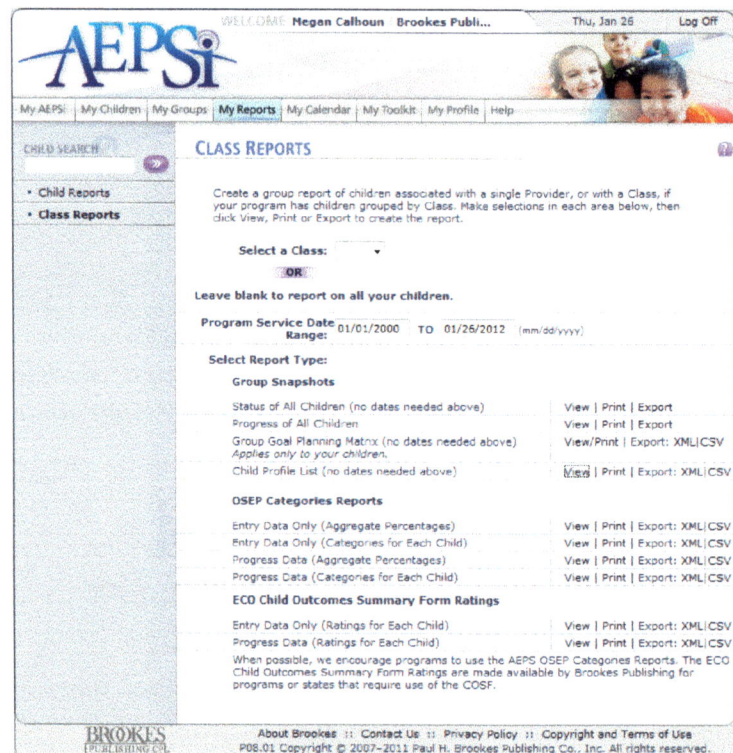

Group Snapshot Reports

Group Snapshots allow you to gauge the status and measure the progress of your children. This enables Providers to better structure their classrooms and focus lessons to meet their children's needs. All of the Group Snapshot reports can be run either by Provider (which would include all children to whom you are assigned) or by Class (which would include all children in a particular classroom).

Status of All Children Report

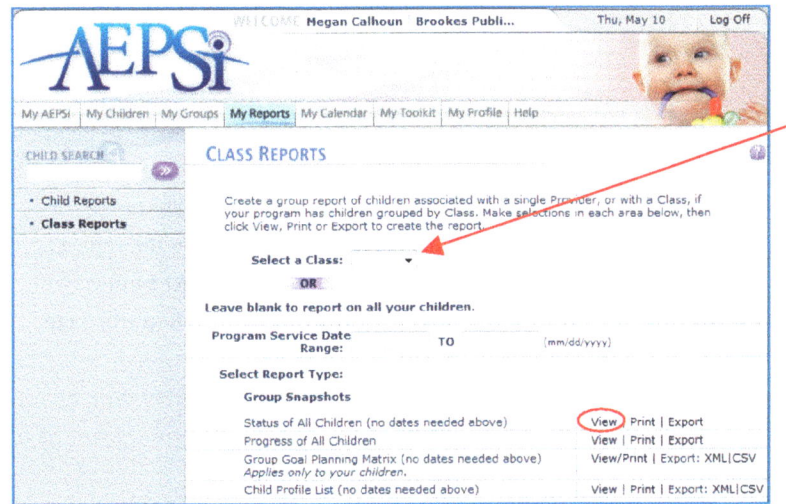

To run a Status of All Children Report, select a classroom from the Class dropdown menu or leave the field blank to run the report on all children assigned to you. Then click the *View* link next the report title from the **Class Reports** page. This report can also be printed or exported.

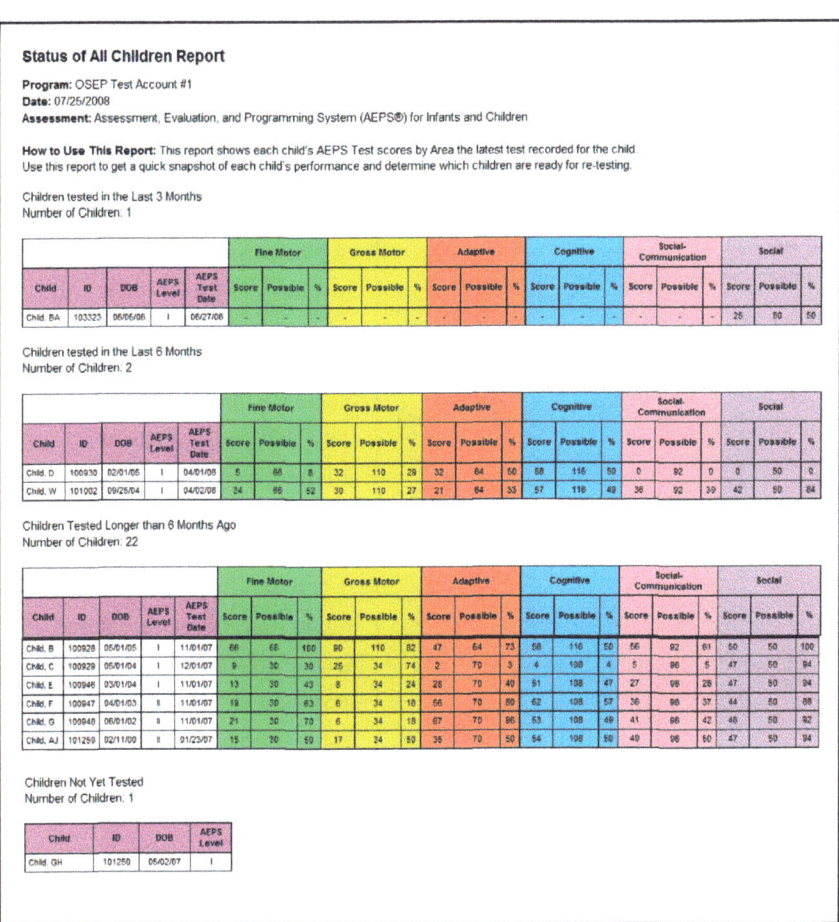

The Status of All Children Report shows each child's AEPS assessment scores, possible score, and percentage score for each of the six areas for that child's most recent assessment.

Children are grouped into 4 categories:
- Those tested in the last 3 months
- Those tested in the last 6 months
- Those tested longer than 6 months ago
- Those not yet tested

This report gives you a quick look at how all of the children are performing and helps you determine which children are ready for retesting.

Progress of All Children Report

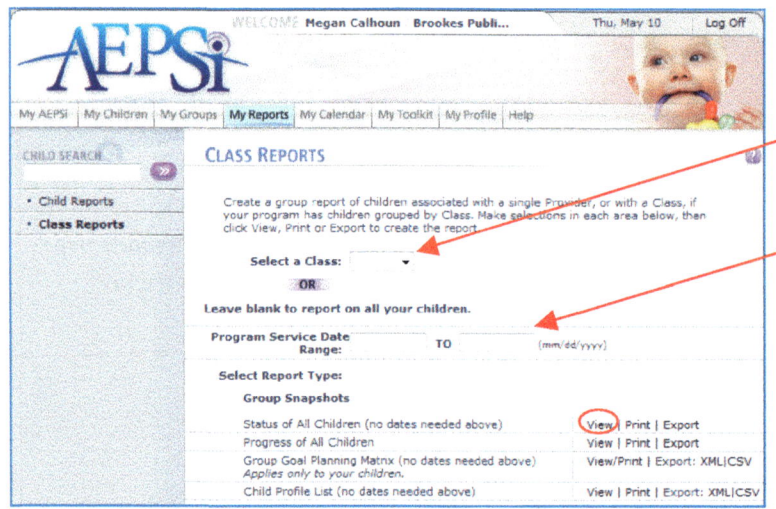

To run a Progress of All Children Report, select a classroom from the Class dropdown menu or leave the field blank to run the report on all children assigned to you. Enter the service date range for which you would like to run the report. Then click the *View* link next to the report title from the **Class Reports** page.

This report can also be printed or exported.

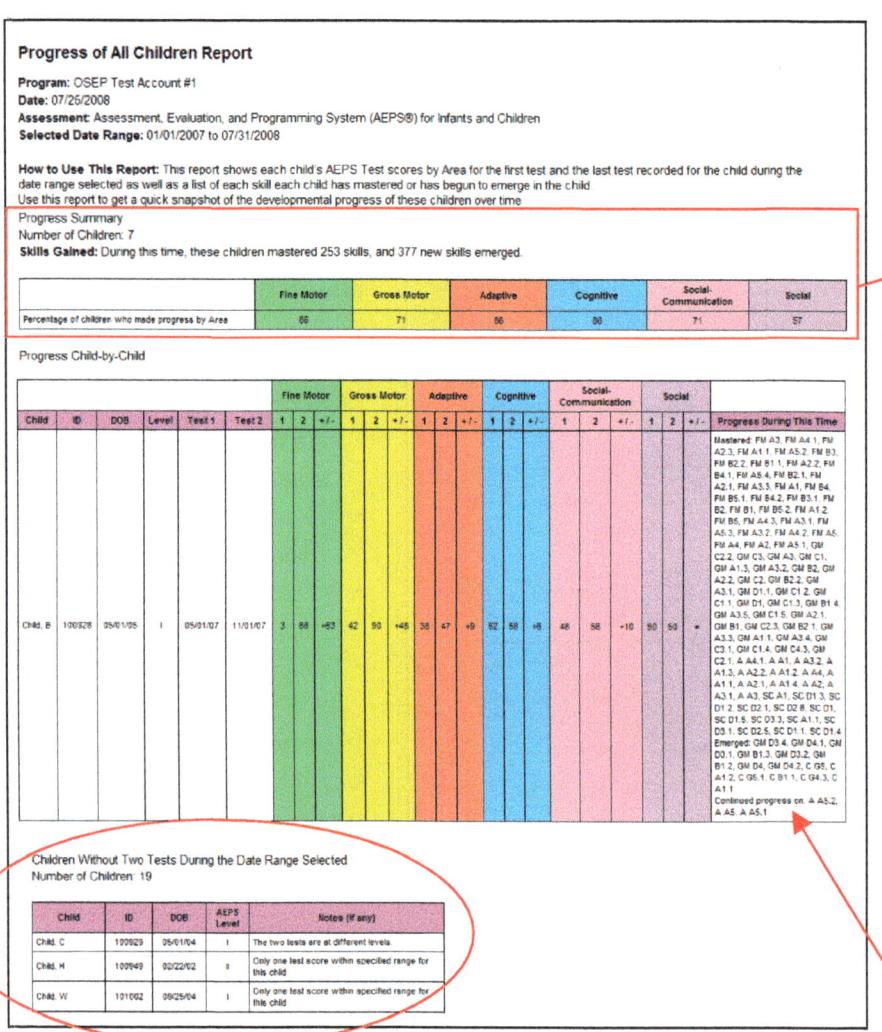

The Progress of All Children Report gives you a quick snapshot of the developmental progress of these children over time.

At the top of the report there is an overall summary, which includes the total number of children included in the report, the number of skills the children mastered, and the number of new skills that emerged for the children, as well as the percentage of children who made progress by area.

Below that, the report shows each child's AEPS assessment scores by area for the first and last test recorded for the child during the date range selected and calculates the increase or decrease between the two assessments.

The report also provides a list of each skill that has been mastered, is emerging, or continued progress on.

At the bottom of the Progress of all Children Report is a list of children who were not included in the report and possible reasons why.

Group Goal Planning Matrix Report

The Group Goal Planning Matrix report shows each child's goals as marked on his or her latest assessments. Use this report to get a quick snapshot of the most critical items to teach, see at a glance which children are working on the same skills, plan individual and group intervention activities, develop embedding schedules, and more.

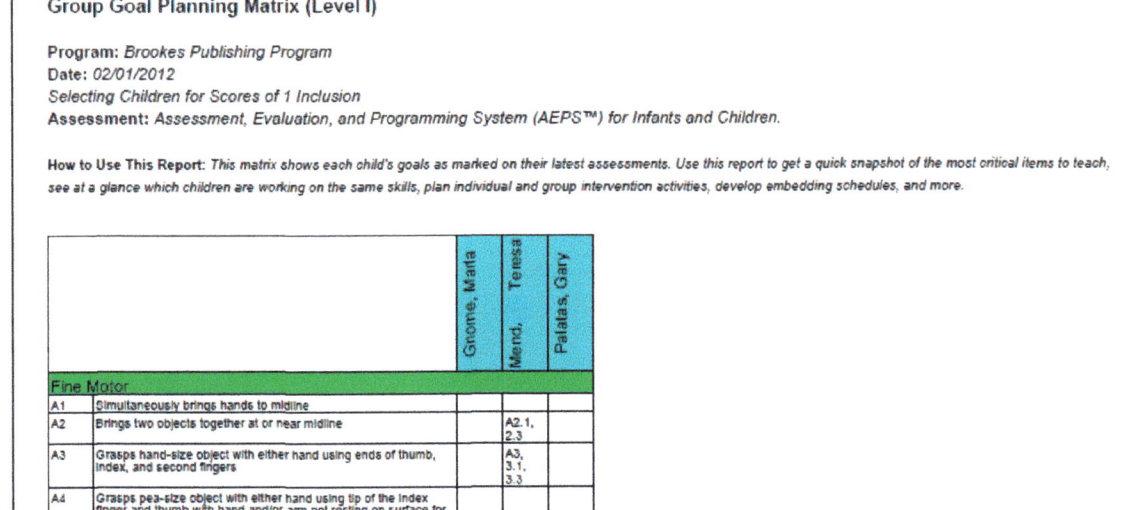

The Group Goal Planning Matrix displays every goal on the AEPS Test in rows and the list of children included in columns. When running the report, you can select one of the following reporting options:

IFSP/IEP: The report will list all AEPS item(s) that were marked for IFSP/IEP on each child's assessment. Use the reporting option to see which children are working on similar goals.

Scores of 1: The report will list all AEPS items that were scored 1 on each child's assessment. Use this reporting option to see which children are emerging in certain skills.

Scores of 0: The report will list all AEPS items that were scored 0 on each child's assessment. Use this reporting option to see which skills have not yet been observed for your children.

Scoring Note A: The report will list all AEPS items that were marked with a scoring note of "A" (Assistance Provided). Use this reporting option to see which children need assistance on similar skills.

Scoring Note B: The report will list all AEPS items that were marked with a scoring note of "B" (Behavior Interfered). Use this reporting option to see which children's behavior interfered on similar skills.

Based on the criteria, the goal and objectives will be displayed for each child. At the end of the report, the names of the children who do not match any of the criteria will be listed, along with their Child IDs and DOBs.

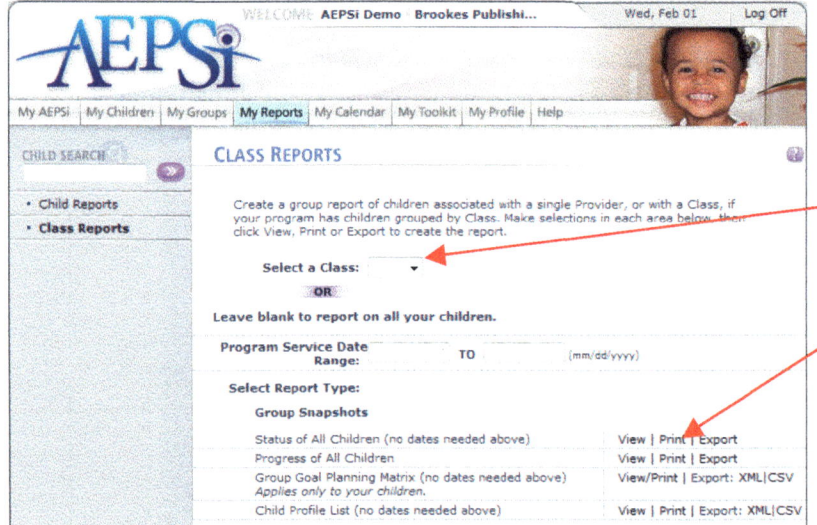

To run a Group Goal Planning Matrix report, select a classroom from the Class dropdown menu or leave the field blank to run the report on all children assigned to you.

Then click the *View/Print* link next to the report title.

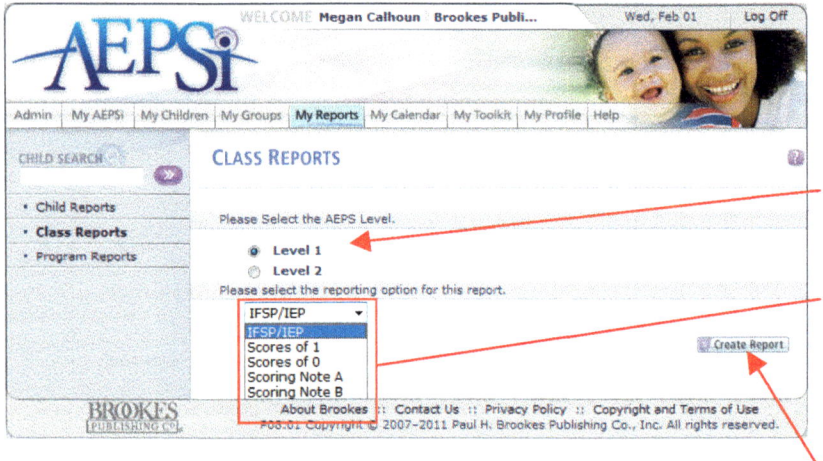

You will be taken to a page where you can choose the AEPS level for the report and select your reporting options.

Select either Level I or Level II for the AEPS level.

Select either IFSP/IEP, Scores of 1, Scores of 0, Scoring Note A, or Scoring Note B from the dropdown menu.

Click the *Create Report* button.

This will open the report in a PDF format. You have the option to print or save the report to your computer. This report is available to export in both XML and CSV formats.

Child Profile List Report

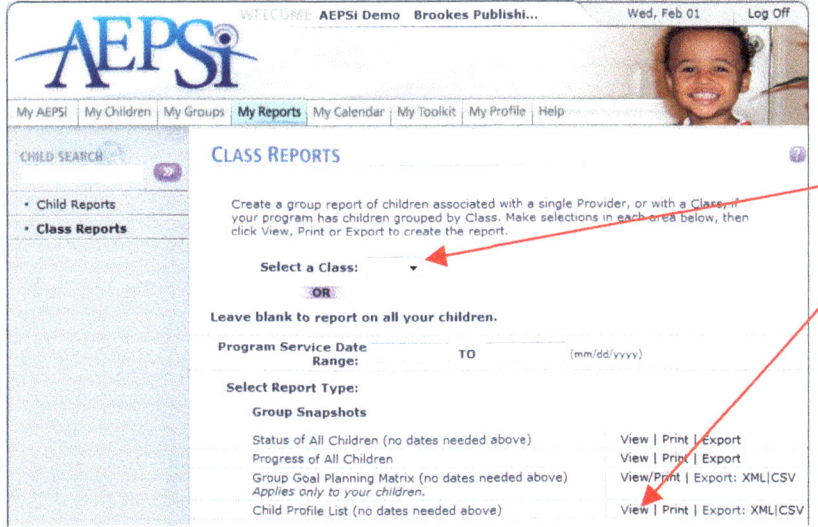

To run a Child Profile List Report, select a classroom from the Class dropdown menu or leave the field blank to run the report on all children assigned to you. Then click the *View* link next the report title.

The Child Profile List Report contains the following demographic information for all children assigned to you, both active and archived:

- Child Name and Child ID
- Child DOB
- Child Status (Active or Archived)
- Gender
- Classroom
- Developmental Status
- Lead Provider
- AEPS level
- Include in OSEP Reporting (Yes or No)
- Funding Source
- Program Entry Date
- Program Exit Date
- Recent Assessment Status

The exported versions of the report (XML or CSV) contain additional useful information, including archived date, number of assessments, and any custom fields that have been created.

OSEP Categories Reports

About OSEP Reporting

AEPSi automatically transforms AEPS Test results into an OSEP report using the crosswalk of AEPS Test items with the three OSEP Child Outcomes and empirically derived same-age-peer benchmarks. AEPS's crosswalk of items correlated to OSEP Child Outcomes has been empirically validated, so you know that your data reported with AEPSi are accurate and genuine. With reliable child outcomes data, you can better tailor interventions to a child's needs and be confident that your entry and exit data will show progress.

To generate the OSEP report, AEPSi:

1. Calculates each child's OSEP outcomes raw scores by gathering and summing children's scores on the specific AEPS Test items that correlate to the three child outcomes required by OSEP
2. Calculates for each child whether or not he or she is performing at the level of same-age peers. Outcome raw scores are compared to empirically validated same-age-peer benchmarks at the appropriate age intervals. Raw scores at or above the benchmarks indicate that a child's performance is similar to same-age peers. Raw scores below the benchmarks indicate that a child's performance is below that of same-age peers.
3. Sorts children into two categories at near entry:
   o Performing as same-age peers
   o Not performing as same-age peers
4. Sorts children into five categories at near exit:
   o Maintained functioning at a level comparable to same-age peers
   o Improved functioning to reach a level comparable to same-age peers
   o Improved functioning to a level nearer to same-age peers but did not reach comparable level
   o Improved functioning but not sufficient to move nearer to functioning comparable to same-age peers
   o Did not improve functioning

There are four OSEP Categories reports that are available in a viewable, printable, and exportable format. The reports are automatically separated by Part B and Part C.

- Entry Data Only (Aggregate Percentages)
- Entry Data Only (Categories for Each Child)
- Progress Data (Aggregate Percentages)
- Progress Data (Categories for Each Child)

> Note: Even though you are no longer required to submit entry data to OSEP, AEPSi still has two entry data reports, which are helpful in determining where children enter the program and monitoring that children receive their entry assessments—which are needed in order to report on progress.

Children on the Alternative Path

Children who are 37 months or older and are still using the Level I test due to severe developmental disabilities are automatically placed on the alternative path for OSEP reporting. At near entry, these children will have an OSEP outcome of not performing as same-age peers. Based on an alternative method, AEPSi will generate OSEP outcomes and recommended ECO ratings. On the Raw Score Reports, the raw score and same-age benchmark will be displayed as n/a.

| Roberts, Damien | 09375 | 07/09/03 | 09/01/06 | 10/13/06 | n/a | n/a | B | n/a | n/a | B | n/a | n/a | B |

There is nothing you need to do in order to place a child on the alternative path. If the child is 37 months or older and a Level I test was used to assess the child, that child will automatically be placed on the alternative path.

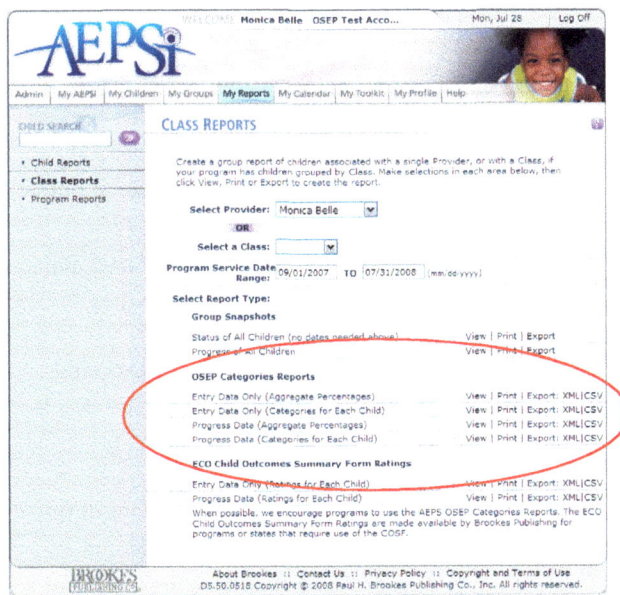

All of the OSEP Categories reports can be run from the **Class Reports** page by selecting a service date range and then clicking the *View* link next to the report you would like to run.

All OSEP Categories reports can also be printed from these pages or exported into XML or CSV files.

Entry Data Only (Aggregate Percentages) Report

The Entry Data Only (Aggregate Percentages) report calculates each child's OSEP outcomes raw scores, compares them to same-age-peer benchmarks, and aggregates the results for each of the three OSEP Child Outcomes.

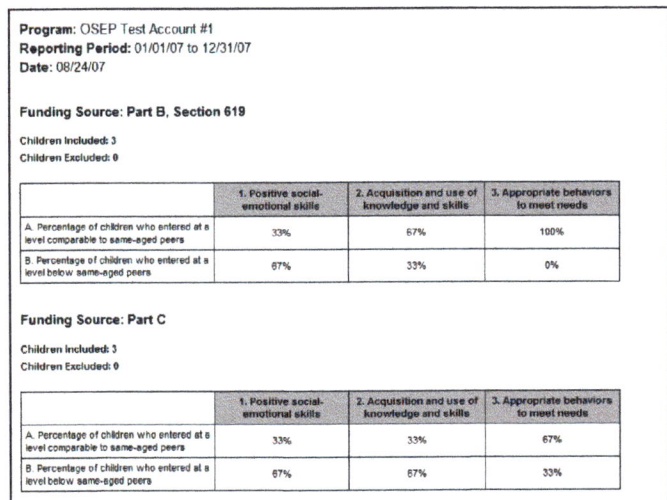

The report displays the percentage of children who are performing at a level comparable to same-age peers and the percentage of children who are not performing at a level comparable to same-age peers.

The results are separated by Part B and Part C, according to the funding source that was selected in the child's profile.

The report also displays the number of children who were included in the report and the number of children who were excluded. More detail on why children were excluded from the report is shown in the Entry Data Only (Categories for Each Child) report.

Entry Data Only (Categories for Each Child) Report

The Entry Data Only (Categories for Each Child) report calculates and displays each child's OSEP outcome raw scores for each of the three OSEP Child Outcomes, the corresponding same-age-peer benchmarks, and whether the child is below or comparable to same-age peers.

In addition, the report displays the child's name, date of birth, program entry date, and the child's age at entry.

The report is separated by Part B and Part C.

A list of children who were excluded from the report and the reason why is also included.

In addition, the export versions of the report (XML and CSV) include any custom fields that have been created.

Progress Data (Aggregate Percentages) Report

The Progress Data (Aggregate Percentages) report calculates each child's OSEP Outcomes raw scores, compares them to their near-entry raw scores and/or same-age-peer benchmarks, and aggregates the results for each of the three OSEP Child Outcomes.

The report displays the percentage of children at near exit who maintained functioning at a level comparable to same-age peers, improved functioning to reach a level comparable to same-age peers, improved functioning to a level nearer to same-age peers but did not reach a comparable level, improved functioning but not sufficient to move nearer to functioning comparable to same-age peers, and did not improve functioning.

The results are separated by Part B and Part C, according to the funding source that was selected in the child profile. The report also displays the number of children who were included in the report and the number of children who were excluded. More information on excluded children is included in the Progress Data (Categories for Each Child) report.

Progress Data (Categories for Each Child) Report

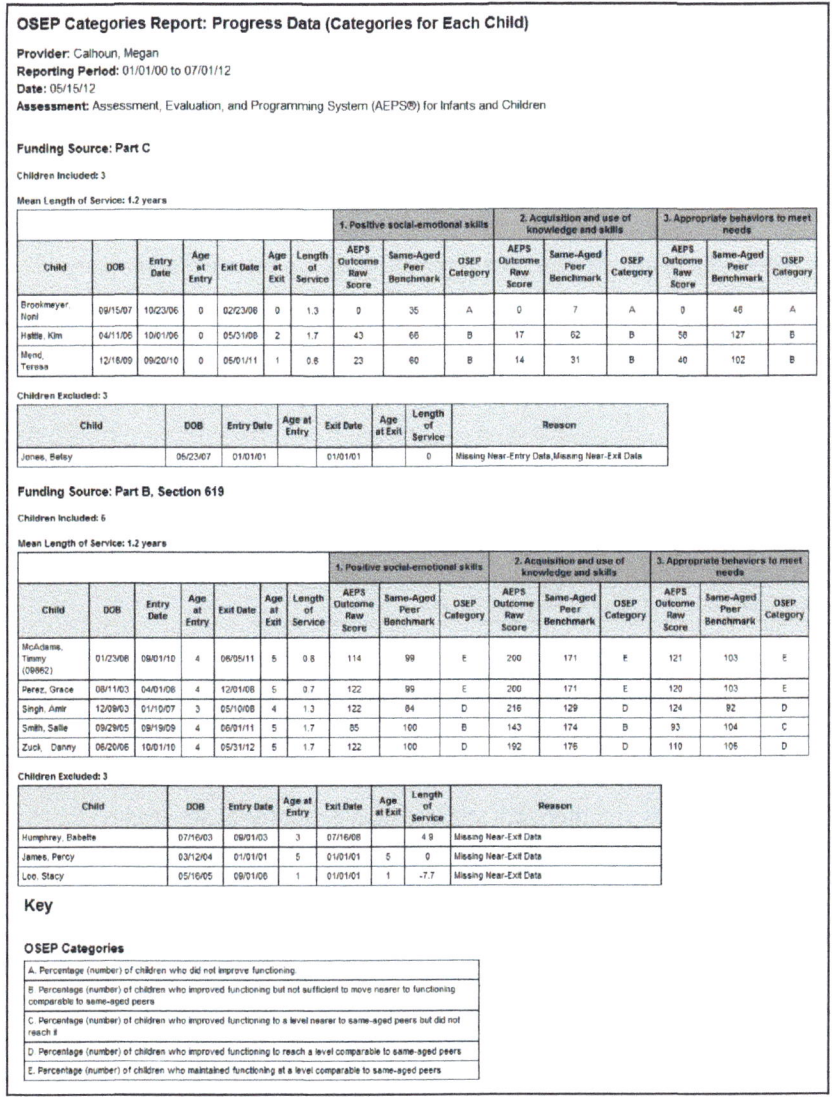

The Progress Data (Categories for Each Child) report calculates and displays each child's OSEP outcome raw scores for each of the three OSEP Child Outcomes, the corresponding same-age-peer benchmarks, and the OSEP Category.

In addition, the report displays the child's name, date of birth, program entry date, age at entry, program exit date, age at exit, and length of service (measured in years).

The report is separated by Part B and Part C.

A list of children who were excluded from the report and the reason why is also included.

In addition, the export versions of the report (XML and CSV) include any custom fields that have been created.

OSEP Report Exclusion Categories

A child may be excluded from an OSEP report due to several reasons. Below is a list of the exclusion categories and what you need to do to correct the error.

Missing Near-Entry Data:

Children Excluded:

Child	ID	DOB	Entry Date	Exit Date	Reason
Abaiye, Oni		07/11/05	10/23/07	10/23/08	Missing Near-Entry Data

Either the near-entry assessment has not been selected for a child or it has not been finalized.

What you should do: Make sure you have selected a near-entry assessment for the child. On the child's summary page, you should see an "OSEP ENTRY" icon next to the assessment you want flagged for near entry. If you do not see the icon, go to the CODRF summary page of the assessment, and select "Near Entry" under the "OSEP Include?" option. Also, verify that the assessment has been finalized and that all test items are complete. See *OSEP Include* in **Section 9: Child Assessments** for more information.

Missing Near-Exit Data:

Children Excluded:

Child	ID	DOB	Entry Date	Exit Date	Reason
Butterfield, Marcy		12/21/03	09/01/04	05/21/08	Missing Near-Exit Data

Either the near-exit assessment has not been selected for a child or it has not been finalized.

What you should do: Make sure you have selected a near-exit assessment for the child. On the child's summary page, you should see an *OSEP EXIT* icon next to the assessment you want flagged for near exit. If you do not see the icon, go to the CODRF summary page of the assessment, and select *Near Exit* under the *OSEP Include?* option. Also, verify that the assessment has been finalized and that all test items are complete. See *OSEP Include* in **Section 9: Child Assessments** for more information.

Less than 6 Months in Services:

Children Excluded:

Child	ID	DOB	Entry Date	Exit Date	Reason
Archer, Lauren	19832	12/15/02	12/16/05	03/01/06	Less than 6 Months in Services

There are less than 6 months between the child's program entry and program exit date. OSEP has mandated that only children who have received services for at least 6 months should be reported on.

What you should do: Go to the child's profile page and verify that you have entered the correct program entry and program exit dates. If you have entered the correct dates and there are still less than 6 months of services received, this child will be excluded from OSEP reporting.

Invalid Funding Source:

Children Excluded:

Child	ID	DOB	Entry Date	Exit Date	Reason
Archer, Lauren	19832	12/15/02	12/16/05	07/01/07	Invalid Funding Source

A funding source other than Part B or Part C has been selected for the child.

What you should do: Go to the child's profile page and verify that either Part B or Part C has been selected for funding source.

Inappropriate Age at Level II Test:

Children Excluded:

Child	ID	DOB	Entry Date	Exit Date	Reason
Archer, Lauren	19832	12/15/00	12/16/05	07/01/07	Inappropriate age at Level II test

If a child is 36 months or younger and is using a Level II test, the inappropriate test was used to assess the child. A Level II test should be used only once a child is older than 36 months and is in the Part B program.

What you should do: Assess the child with the age-appropriate test.

ECO Child Outcomes Summary Form Ratings

There are two ECO Child Outcomes Summary Form Ratings, one with near-entry data only and one with progress data.

These reports can be run from the **Class Reports** page by selecting the service date range and then clicking the *View* link next to the report you would like to run.

The ECO Child Outcomes Summary Form Ratings can also be printed or exported into either XML or CSV files.

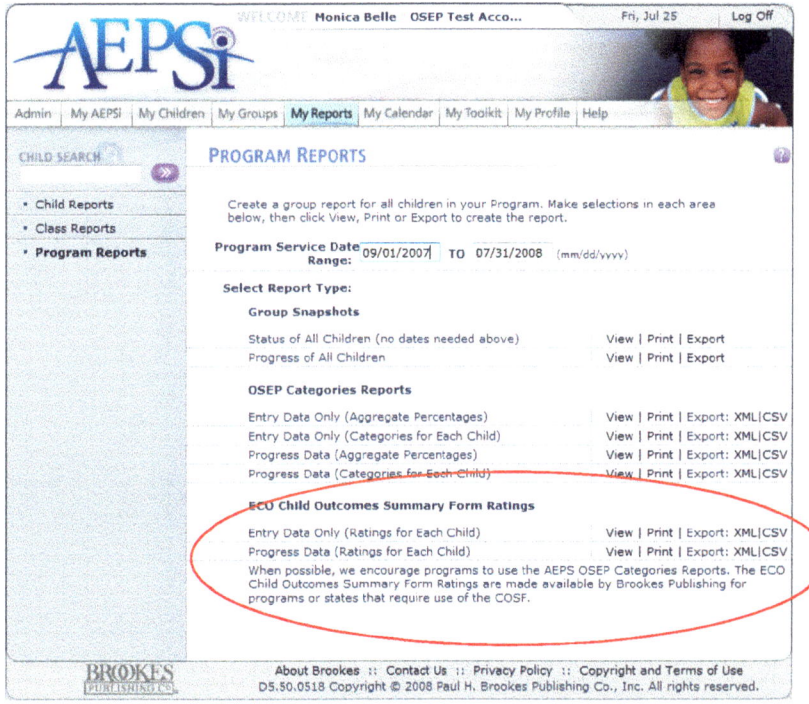

Entry Data Only (Ratings for Each Child) Report

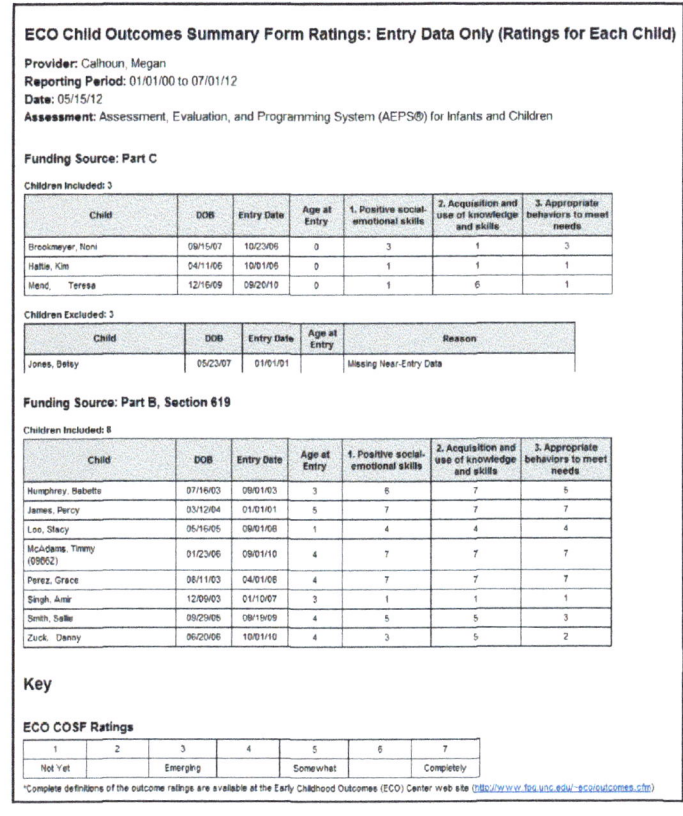

For those programs that require use of the COSF, AEPSi provides a recommended ECO Rating for each child using the 1 to 7 scale. The report displays the child's name, date of birth, program entry date, age at entry, and the recommended ECO rating for each of the three outcomes.

were excluded from the report and the reason why.

In addition, the export versions of the report (XML and CSV) include any custom fields that have been created.

Progress Data (Ratings for Each Child) Report

The Progress Data ECO Ratings report displays the recommended ECO ratings for near entry and near exit and indicates whether progress occurred (Y for yes, N for no).

Also included in the report are the child's name, date of birth, program entry date, age at entry, program exit date, age at exit, and length of service (measured in years).

A list of children who were excluded from the report and the reason why is displayed as well.

In addition, the export versions of the report (XML and CSV) include any custom fields that have been created.

My Toolkit

Section 15

My Toolkit is an area within AEPSi that includes useful information for you as a Provider, including News & Updates, Downloads & Resources, a Discussion Board, resources for Professional Development, and the AEPSi Curriculum Reference Guides.

Click the **My Toolkit** tab on the upper taskbar to access all the items within **My Toolkit**.

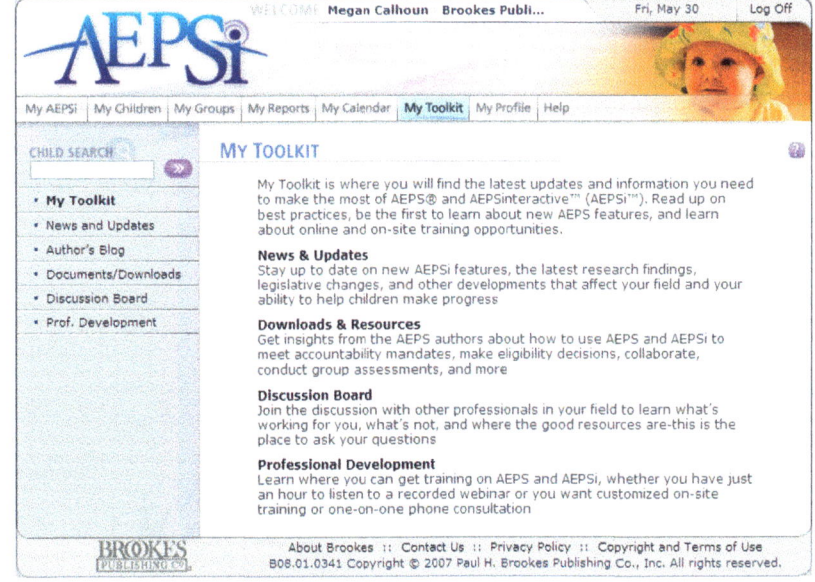

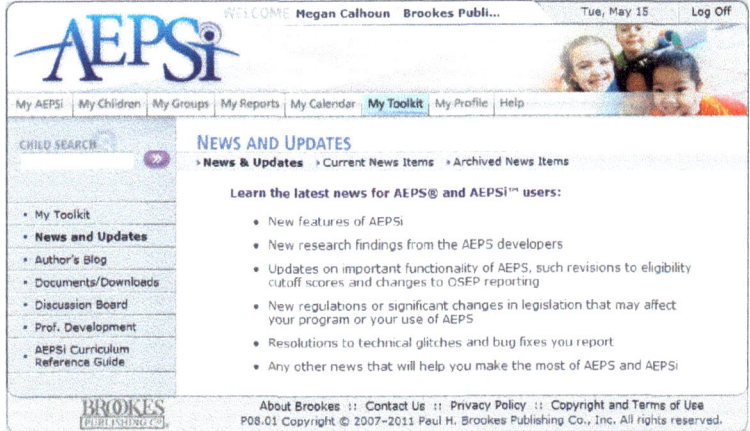

In the **News & Updates** section, you can find announcements, updates, and bug fixes related to the AEPSi application.

The **Documents & Downloads** section contains a collection of useful documents, including the State Standards Correlations, the AEPS/OSEP Crosswalk, and white papers from the authors of AEPS, as well as other documents and downloadable resources.

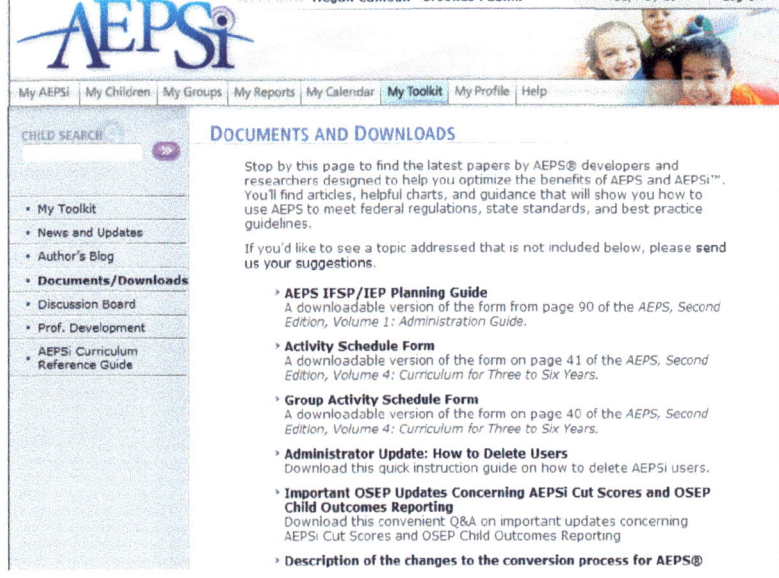

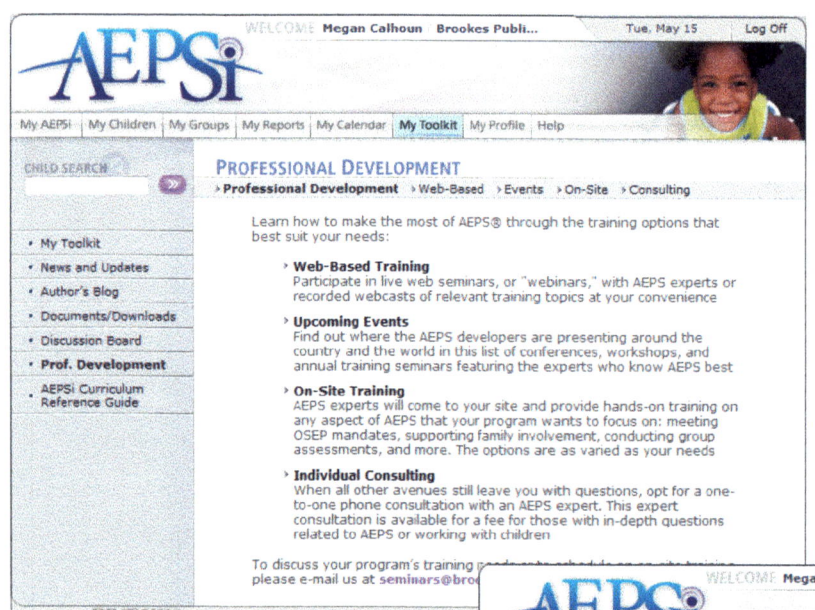

In the **Professional Development** section, you can find detailed information about content consulting, live training, and web-based training options, including webcasts and webinars.

In the **AEPSi Curriculum Reference Guide** section, you can access interactive tools that allow you to locate activity-based interventions, sample teaching tactics, instructional sequences, recommendations for environmental arrangements, and strategies for incorporating the activities into the child's daily routines from the AEPS curriculum.

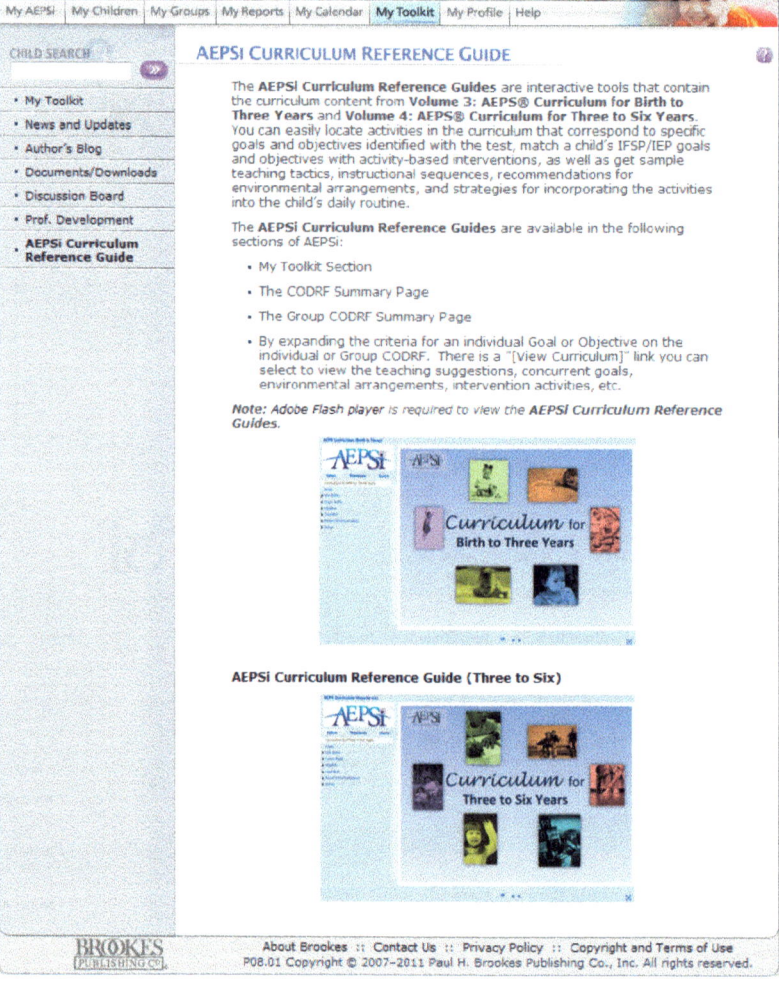

My Profile

Section 16

The **My Profile** page is the page within AEPSi that includes your personal information. You may view or edit your profile at any time by clicking the **My Profile** tab at the top of your screen.

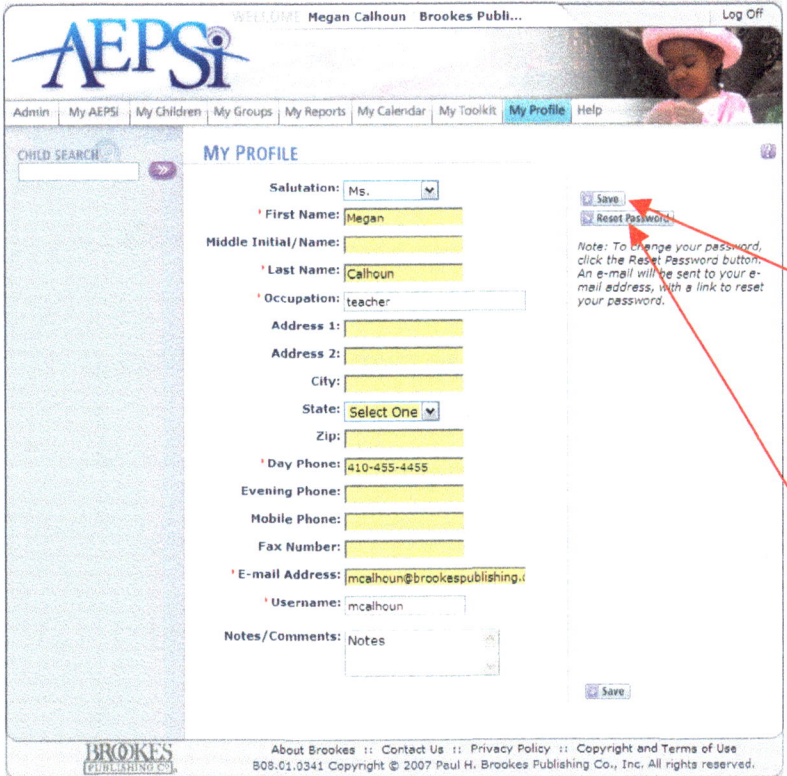

Editing My Profile

You may add or change your personal information by clicking inside the text boxes next to the profile fields and typing in the information.

Click the *Save* button to save your information.

You may also reset your password at any time by clicking the *Reset Password* button on your profile page.

AEPSi Provider Guide | 53

Help

Section 17

The **Help** section of AEPSi is dedicated to helping you understand how to use AEPSi. This section includes a list of Frequently Asked Questions (FAQs), the AEPSi User Manual, a Getting Started Tutorial, and a sitemap of AEPSi.

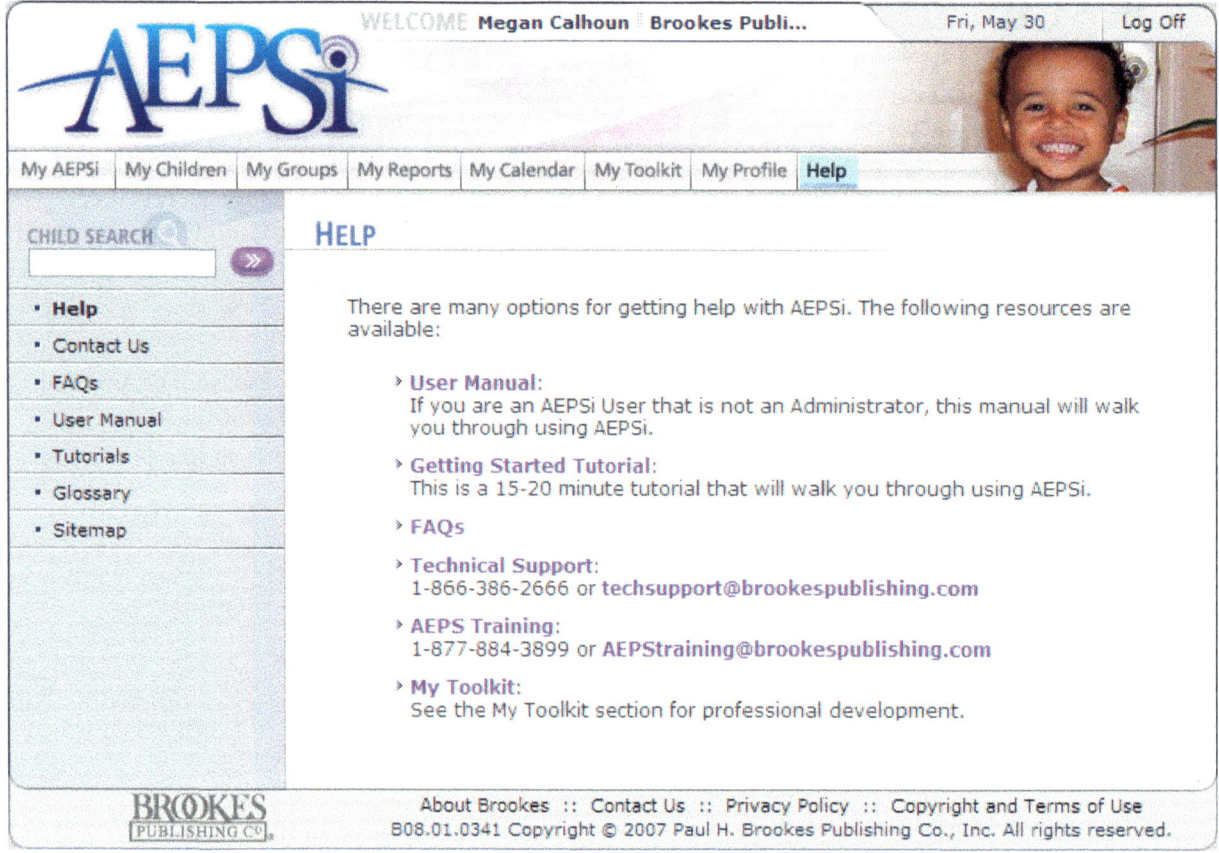